# Chaim Walder

# People Speak 3

## Everyone has a story...

Translated by Yocheved Lavon

FELDHEIM PUBLISHERS
JERUSALEM  NEW YORK

Originally published in Hebrew as *Anashim Mesaprim al Atzmam 3*

The following stories were translated by Chani Goldwasser:
A Match Made in Heaven, Lifesaver, Return to Sender, Ears to Hear

ISBN 978-1-59826-175-2

Edited and typeset by Eden Chachamtzedek

FELDHEIM PUBLISHERS
POB 43163 / Jerusalem, Israel

208 Airport Executive Park
Nanuet, NY 10954

www.feldheim.com

10  9  8  7  6  5  4  3  2  1

*Printed in Israel*

# Contents

# A Heart of Gold

W hen my husband and I got married fifteen years ago, our families provided for us beautifully. Each side gave all it could. They made a lovely wedding for us, and they bought us a nice apartment.

A few days before the wedding, my *chasan*'s grandmother came to see me, bringing a gift. I knew it wasn't going to be just any old gift. This was a special ritual in their family, and very soon, I found out why.

She opened her bag and took out a little package. I unwrapped it, opened the box, and before my eyes I beheld a gorgeous diamond ring.

I don't know much about diamonds, but I didn't have to be an expert to see that this must have cost a lot of money. It was the biggest diamond I'd ever seen.

My family gathered around me and began oohing and aahing. "This is my wedding gift to you," said my *chasan*'s grandmother simply.

Afterwards I learned that she buys an expensive piece of jewelry for *every kallah* who joins the family — in order to be remembered, I guess — since it's the sort of thing a woman treasures and wears all her life.

To tell you the truth, I really didn't need a present like this in order to remember my *chasan*'s grandmother. She was a wonderful, sweet, noble-spirited lady, and everybody loved her just for herself. But this was the family custom, and who am I to quibble with such a custom — especially when receiving a five-thousand-dollar diamond ring?

Yes, that's how much it cost. How do I know that? You'll soon see.

After Grandma had left, my father's reaction was to ask how anyone could go around wearing a ring like that when people are out in the streets, homeless and hungry. But he would have said the same thing if the ring had cost five hundred dollars, so I wasn't insulted. But on the other hand, it did bother my conscience to wear such an expensive ring. And it bothered me in other ways, too — ways that only a woman would understand.

I don't want to sound like a fussy person, but the ring was too big for me. I mean the band, not the diamond. Not much too big, just a little bit loose. Ask any woman and she'll tell you how annoying it is to have a ring that feels like it's constantly falling off. You have to keep checking to make sure it's still there.

All through the wedding, that's what I was doing. I kept pushing that ring back up on my finger. Finally I put my wedding ring on top of it, to hold it in place, but I kept feeling it rattling against the wedding ring.

Aside from that, the wedding was wonderful, and so was the week of *Sheva Berachos*. For Shabbos, my family hosted the meals, and we had my husband's family staying with us. The

Shabbos evening meal was delightful, with lively songs and touching speeches, and the morning meal was just as enjoyable. After the meal, we went out for a walk. Since we live in Netanya, near the seashore, we walked along the beach.

After *Minchah* we had the third Shabbos meal, which continued until *motza'ei Shabbos*. The men went to *daven Maariv*, and afterwards, my husband made *Havdalah* for everyone. As is customary when a *chasan* makes his first *Havdalah*, everyone threw pillows at him — which is meant to give him a good excuse if he stumbles over the words, thus saving him from embarrassment.

And so Shabbos ended.

Suddenly, someone asked me, "Where's your ring?"

I looked at my hand, and to my horror, the diamond ring was gone. I turned pale and felt like I was going to faint.

Everyone looked at my empty finger in shock. A small uproar broke out, with everyone talking at once.

We all started looking around the house, checking under the furniture and in the crevices of the living-room couch. Someone even went through the garbage to make sure that it hadn't accidentally been thrown away.

By now, every member of the family knew that I'd lost a ring that cost five thousand dollars. (And that's why I know how much it cost. When you lose something, suddenly everyone starts announcing how much it's worth.)

Then, my mother-in-law, together with a few aunts, went up to the guest room we were using, and to my intense mortification, started going through our suitcases. I had left the room much messier than usual. That, compounded with the fact they were rummaging through all my personal items, made me want to sink into the floor.

After unsuccessfully searching the house for about an hour, my mother said, "Maybe you forgot it at home?"

"I'll run home and look for it," my husband quickly volunteered. He took one of his brothers with him and raced out the door. We lived about a twenty-minute drive from my parents' home, so I knew it would take at least an hour before he'd be back. I waited anxiously, nibbling at my nails.

Something told me that he wasn't going to be successful in his quest. That "something" had a lot to do with the fact that I was sure I had put it on before Shabbos, yet I couldn't recall feeling that annoying sensation of a loose ring on my finger for hours. And that didn't bode well for my diamond ring — or for me.

I feared the worst, and that's what happened next. My husband came back and said, "I couldn't find it."

"Did you look on the night table?"

"Yes."

"Did you look in the chest of drawers?"

"Yes."

"Did you look in the kitchen? By the bathroom sink?"

He'd looked everywhere, but the ring was nowhere to be found.

Everyone sat down in the living room and began suggesting various possibilities as to what might have happened. At this point I mentioned, with some trepidation, that the ring was a little too big.

"Well, why didn't you say so at the time?" one of the aunts asked icily.

I replied that as a matter of fact, I had said so. My in-laws exchanged knowing glances.

We tried to reconstruct the events of the day, and came to the conclusion that most likely the ring was somewhere in the sand on the beach.

Now, even if I'd dropped it in a sandbox, it would be a little hard to find; so to find it along the seashore beside Netanya, well, that would be practically impossible.

Everyone just stared at me. No one attempted to comfort me; no one said it wasn't my fault. I can understand how they felt. It was really a very expensive ring. I guess I should have been happy that they weren't yelling at me, "What's wrong with you? Aren't you old enough and responsible enough to be trusted to take care of a five-thousand-dollar ring?" True, they weren't yelling, but those words were written all over their faces.

My husband and I went home very downhearted. He tried to lighten things up with a joke: "This is a lucky break for me! Now I can lose something valuable and it won't matter."

His joke cost him dearly, because I thought he was being sarcastic. All the anger I was feeling towards myself now erupted against him.

Shocked that I had exploded that way, he apologized over and over again, saying that he hadn't meant to rub salt on the wound, but I was hurt to the depths of my soul. Not only did I feel guilty about losing the ring, I felt terribly offended at the way his family had tacitly tried to make me feel even worse — at least that's how it seemed to me.

My husband behaved with true nobility. He comforted me, and said that the person who was really to blame was the one who had told me to wear the ring even though it was too big. He even tried to blame himself for not realizing that such a thing could happen. That was so good of him. That night, I privately acknowledged that if this had been a test, he had passed it.

Okay, so my husband passed the test, but his family certainly didn't.

Every time we met, the subject of the ring seemed to hover in the air. Someone would ask how I was feeling about the loss, or mention that no one had dared to tell Grandma about it, but that she'd probably figured it out for herself and was suffering in silence. Many more jabs of this sort made me feel miserable.

I can't really blame them. Apparently, that's just how people are. If you lose something of value, you pay a price for it — a much higher price, I might add, than the worth of the item. You could say that along with the ring, I lost their esteem and affection. How can you like a person who's so irresponsible that after only a week she has already lost such an expensive ring? What is she, a little girl?

Usually the jabs didn't come as outright attacks — only as hints here and there. But if I tried to defend myself, explaining how it had really been too big, then they really came down on me. At first they'd shake their heads sympathetically and say, "What a pity. Just a size too big…" And then they'd snap back with, "But why weren't you more careful with it then?!"

This went on for months. I felt as if I'd never win back their respect. It was as if I'd been permanently branded as irresponsible and unreliable.

However, the breaking point came one day when we were at his parents' house for a family gathering, during which my in-laws gave us a beautiful present — a very expensive vase. As we were about to leave, one of my brothers-in-law said to my husband, "You'd better be sure to carry it yourself," casting a meaningful glance in my direction, which everyone seemed to have picked up on.

I have never been so insulted and offended in my entire life as I was at that moment. All the anger and hurt that I had swallowed over the months came bursting out. I told them that I wouldn't set foot in their house ever again, and that they were killing me — and quite a few other things, as well. I must say they were taken aback to hear these things coming out of my mouth. Quite honestly, so was I.

The situation developed into a real rift in the family. My poor husband was caught in the middle. He tried confronting his siblings, explaining to them how hurt I was by all the barbs, but they said that they were also insulted by my outburst.

At that point, his Grandma found out that we'd had a falling out and decided to intervene. Consequently, she had to acknowledge that she knew the whole story. Her mediation brought about a sort of forced reconciliation, with both sides saying all the awkward things that are usually said in these situations. My mother-in-law apologized for offending me and said that I was actually her favorite daughter-in-law, and I asked her forgiveness for yelling at them.

Frankly, I was tired of the whole business. There was peace, but it was a chilly sort of peace. I was sure I'd lost all hope of ever coming back into their good graces. They would never really respect me, they would never love me, and they certainly would never entrust me with anything costing three digits or more.

The turning point came four months later.

I haven't yet mentioned that our wedding took place two days after Shavuos, and that my husband, like many other Israeli *yeshivah bachurim*, wore a long frock coat for the wedding and the week of *Sheva Berachos*. When the festivities were over and our everyday life began, the frock coat was retired to the closet, to be worn only on holidays.

Summer went by, and Rosh Hashanah came. On the eve of the holiday, it was time to take out the frock coat again. When my husband put it on, he turned to me and asked if it still fit him all right. Maybe he'd put on some weight?

I lied, may Hashem forgive me, and said he looked as slim as ever.

He began patting his chest with the strangest expression on his face. I got a bit scared and wondered if I should run to call an ambulance.

Then he reached into the breast pocket of the frock coat, and guess what he pulled out?

We both stared at the ring in shocked silence for a long moment.

"I can't believe it," he said. "I must have put it in my jacket pocket some time during the week of *Sheva Berachos.*"

I took the ring from his hand and began to cry. I don't know whether it was from the excitement of finding the ring, or the release of four months of pent-up tension.

My husband called his mother right away to tell her the news; he sounded as if we'd just had our first child.

When Rosh Hashanah was over, we were inundated with a stream of visitors. They all wanted to see it with their own eyes. His parents came and goggled at the ring, his siblings came, and then Grandma and Grandpa themselves came, all smiles.

Everyone breathed a sigh of relief, and they all asked me to forgive them for thinking I was irresponsible, and in the same breath they wondered out loud why it hadn't occurred to them that my husband might have misplaced it. He was known in the family for his forgetfulness. Maybe he was a bit insulted, but the joy of finding the ring more than made up for it.

From then on, I was the darling of the family. They all

saw how mistaken they'd been. To them I became a very responsible person, who'd never lost a thing in her life and was gracious enough to marry their son and brother despite his lack of responsibility. All this added additional points to my credit.

Suddenly, I was barraged with tons of love and thousands of apologies. My husband was happy for me, even though it was painful for him to become the target of all the blame. What really mattered was what he'd gained: a happy wife and harmony in the home.

But the story didn't end there.

I'm afraid I bore a bit of a grudge against my husband for everything I'd suffered because of him. All those months that we'd thought *I* was the one who'd lost the ring, he'd never used it against me, but when the tables were turned, I wasn't as good as he was.

I was always finding ways of reminding him. If he had to go to the bank with a large sum of cash, or was carry anything of value, I'd say to him, "You'd better let someone else take it, so it won't get lost in a sandbox." The word "sandbox" became sort of a symbolic expression that I'd use to remind him of his guilt.

I'm ashamed of the way I acted, but I think it's something that unfortunately many people do. They use other people's weaknesses against them, hurting those who are closest and most dear to them. It's definitely forbidden by the Torah, but that, I confess, is what I did.

Yet my husband never complained. Sometimes I would notice a pained expression on his face, and then I would feel sorry and apologize to him. But beyond that, he never made an issue of it.

Our life proceeded normally. We have seven wonderful children who love and honor their parents. Some of them, I think, have heard the family story of the lost ring, the one everyone thought Mommy had lost, until in the end it turned out it was really Tatty, who had it in his frock-coat pocket all the time....

Fifteen years passed.

Grandma was already in a better world, but her ring remained. Every time I wore it to a *simchah* and received compliments on it from other women, I remembered her — just as she'd hoped I would.

But one day, I began to get a hankering for some new jewelry, and I thought perhaps I'd see about trading in that ring for some new pieces. I wanted to surprise my husband, so I said nothing to him and asked my mother-in-law where Grandma used to buy jewelry. She told me the name of a certain well-known jeweler, and as soon as I had a chance, I went to him.

"This was purchased here," I said, showing him the ring, "and I'd like you to tell me how much it's worth."

He peered at the stone through his jeweler's glass, let out an admiring whistle, and said, "This is quite a valuable diamond. It's worth at least six thousand dollars. I'm willing to take it in exchange for whatever you choose, but just to set the record straight, it was not purchased here. This isn't the kind of stone I would forget."

"But it *was* bought here," I insisted, mentioning Grandma's name. "She was a regular customer of yours, wasn't she?"

"She was. But I'm sure I never sold her this. This, she bought somewhere else."

Suddenly it occurred to me that if this diamond was worth more than six thousand, maybe it was worth even seven. I'd better consult with my husband after all, I said to myself.

I went home and decided to look for the certificate that had been given with the purchase of the stone. All the warranties and documents pertaining to the expensive pieces that I owned were kept in a manila envelope in a little safe.

It didn't take long to find the certificate and the receipt for the diamond. I saw that the jeweler was right; this particular stone had been bought from another dealer. The price was five thousand dollars...that was interesting. According to the jeweler's appraisal, then, the stone's value had really increased.

Just as I was starting to put the documents away, one little detail on the receipt caught my eye, something that I wouldn't have otherwise noticed.

I waited until my husband came home from work. It was almost time. My heart was pounding.

When he arrived, I told him I'd been thinking of trading in the ring for some new pieces, and that I'd gone to Grandma's jeweler and had it appraised.

After I told him how much it was worth, he said, "Great, so we make a profit."

"Yes," I said, "but the jeweler said he wasn't the one who sold it to Grandma. He said he couldn't have forgotten such a stone, and she definitely bought it elsewhere."

"*Nu*," said my husband, "that's possible."

"Could it be that even though she always bought her jewelry at his store, she went to another dealer when she wanted to buy a gift for me?"

"Well, why not? What's the problem?"

17

"I'll tell you what the problem is," I said. "The problem is that for fifteen years I haven't had any idea what a wonderful man I'm married to. You did it in the most…the most beautiful way possible. *I* lost the ring, and you went, and quietly, behind the scenes — I don't know how you did it, you must have taken out loans — you bought me a new ring! Don't try to deny it; I know. You put it over very well. You found a ring that looked just like it, and for the same price…but one thing gave you away. The date."

I placed the receipt before his eyes. It was dated in September of the year we were married. "Grandma bought the ring before the wedding, and that was in June. This ring was purchased at least four months after she bought the original," I said, bursting into tears.

What a gift he had given me! A young man, taking a debt of thousands of dollars upon himself in order to make his family think he, and not his wife, was at fault. I'm sure I was the first woman to receive a gift like that, and I don't mean the ring. I mean the fifteen years of guilt that he lifted from me and bore on his own shoulders. And how he bore it! I still cringe every time I remember the stinging remarks I had made over the years.

Since it was all out in the open, he told me about the hardships he'd gone through paying off those loans. He'd realized that he could never put things right between his family and me unless he made them believe that I wasn't the guilty party. "They're good people," he told me, "but good people have their weak points, too, and this was theirs."

It took years for him to get out of debt, and all that time he had to put up with my little jabs. But it was those jabs that told him his deed had been worthwhile, for they showed him his wife was in good spirits. On the whole, our life ticked along harmoniously.

I learned a tremendous lesson, and I want to pass along part of it to your readers: Never, ever, remind someone of his weakness. Certainly don't use it against him. And even if you don't taunt a person who has made a mistake, you may still harbor anger towards him. Nothing is worth the pain and sorrow that can result from such a situation. Throw all your jewels in the garbage, but don't make people feel bad over them.

My husband had the heroism to bear my guilt for fifteen years, with one goal in mind: that his wife should feel good. He was like Rabbi Yochanan, who said, "It is better for a man to throw himself into a flaming furnace rather than shame his fellow man in public."

This started out as the story of a diamond ring, but it's really the story of a heart of gold.

# *The Keyboard Player*

I play the keyboard and, for the most part, I'm hired to play at small *simchah*s. You won't see me at weddings, because for weddings people hire a whole band, or one of those high-tech keyboard players whose hardware system *sounds like* a whole band. I'd like to think that I play well, but I can't pretend to come anywhere near those musicians who manage, with their ten fingers, to make their keyboards sound like a ten-man band.

So I play at celebrations like bar mitzvahs, *Sheva Berachos*, engagement parties, and even at birthday parties that people make for their kids. You might be surprised, but I've managed to make a pretty good living this way. I don't need very expensive amplifying equipment that's used for weddings. At small *simchah*s you don't have the teenagers who come up and tell you to raise the volume, or the old fellows who subsequently threaten to report you to the police, City Hall, and the Environmental Protection Agency for polluting the atmosphere with all those decibels. I play at second-rate *simchah*s in third-rate halls.

By working this way, you can make two or three hundred dollars in an evening. If you work about ten gigs a month, you've got enough to get through the month nicely, because you have very little overhead. You don't have any other musicians to pay, and if you're not lazy, you can carry the amplifiers in by yourself — so you don't even need a kid to help you. And besides, it leaves you plenty of time for other things.

The work has its disadvantages, though. You get home late at night, all tired out. And often, you have to miss other people's *simchahs*.

As long as we're on the subject of disadvantages, excuse me for digressing, but the biggest disadvantage is having to deal with the guys who think they can sing. They come up and ask for the microphone to sing along with my playing. This doesn't happen too often at weddings, but at bar mitzvahs and *Sheva Berachos*, where the atmosphere is more casual, they do it a lot.

I guess you're thinking that it must be pretty hard to take — and you're right. You might say it sounds as bad as it sounds. Having to accompany a guy who's singing off-key is the worst thing that can happen to a musician. It hurts your ears and makes your head spin, and it gives you the feeling that you're the one who's off-key. And if it's some screechy little kid who's performing this torture session and you try to stop him in the middle, you can be sure his mother will come along and set you straight. She'll even make sure you play another song with him, to make it up to him.

So you learn to suffer in silence, and you let them all have the microphone: the bar mitzvah boy, and then all his cousins and friends — not to mention his great uncle, who has never had the chance until now to show what a talented *chazzan* he is, because they never let him lead the *davening* in shul.

21

Sometimes, a real catastrophe occurs: the bar mitzvah boy, or his neighbor, wants to play on my keyboard. Do you realize what that means? My beloved instrument, that I take such good care of, is about to suffer abuse. But you know what? I let them do it. I don't stand guard, trying to protect it; I run and hide. Maybe it's because I have sensitive ears, or maybe I'm just too ashamed to look my keyboard in the face.

One day, someone called me on the phone and said, "I'm marrying off a daughter, and I'd like you to play at the *Sheva Berachos.*"

Before I even asked his name, I knew who it was. He had been a counselor in the after-school learning group I used to go to more than thirty-five years earlier. He'd been in charge of hundreds of boys over the years, and no doubt he'd forgotten me.

But I remembered him *very* well. I had the kind of run-in with him that isn't so easily forgotten. One day I indulged in a little misbehavior while the group was studying. He asked me a question and I gave him a smart-alecky answer. He picked up a steel ruler and told me to fold up the fingers of my right hand. Then he grabbed my hand and started hitting it hard with the ruler. At first I just looked at him in stunned silence. But when I saw that he wasn't stopping, I tried to pull my hand away. But he held it tightly and continued hitting me. I pleaded with him to stop. I was hopping up and down in pain, yet he went right on hitting me. I started to feel dizzy — not only from the physical pain, but from the terrible humiliation of it all. Not one of the other boys tried to help me — probably because they were afraid he'd hit them, too.

To this day, when I recall that incident, I feel pity for that kid, jumping and sobbing and begging for mercy. It never even occurred to the counselor that while he was hitting his body, he was leaving scars on his soul. And when I remember that *I* was that kid, my pity gives way to rage.

When I went home that day, I hid my injured hand in my pocket. I was too ashamed to tell my parents how I'd been humiliated in front of dozens of other boys.

It took three weeks for the physical wounds to heal, but the psychological wounds were still there thirty-five years later. Maybe I could exaggerate and say that incident ruined my life, or all sorts of other things that people say in order to rationalize their failures and shortcomings. The truth is, though, it didn't ruin my life; I was successful in my field. But I'd never forgotten what happened to me — never.

And suddenly, thirty-five years later, this counselor pops up out of the blue and says I should come and play for him. The same fingers that were swollen and bruised from those merciless blows should make music for him, for this man who never should have been given authority over children.

⌨        ⌨        ⌨

I wanted to say to him, "I know who you are, and I'm not interested in contributing to your *simchah*. You ought to be glad I'm not planning to come down there and tell all your guests what you did to me back then!"

But I couldn't bring those words to my lips. My parents raised me to always speak politely to my elders, even if they don't deserve it. I didn't want to have any dealings with him, though, so I decided to get rid of him by quoting a high price.

"It'll cost you five hundred dollars," I said.

"Five hundred! Everyone else charges half that amount!"

I was starting to get angry. "That is my price, sir. If it suits you, fine. If not, you can look for another musician."

We both hung up and I thought that was the last I was going to hear from him. But fifteen minutes later he called again. "All right," he said. "I'll give you five hundred, then."

I was in shock. I didn't know whether to be mad at myself for leaving him an opening, or to be glad that I would be making twice as much as usual for an evening's work. I decided to look at the bright side.

Everything was surprisingly comfortable for me. The hall was near my house, and the whole affair was pretty short and free of any off-key talent-show artists. At the end of the evening, the bride's father took out five hundred dollars from his pocket, paid me, thanked me, and said good night.

About six months later, he called me again. This time, too, I felt like telling him to find someone else. I had a good mind to tell him who I was. But to tell you the truth, I was feeling a little less angry with him by then, although I was still upset enough to try and put him off with my price.

"Five hundred dollars," I said.

"Reb *Yid*, you're expensive," he sighed. "But you're good. I like the way you play, and I'll take you."

Things went on this way for two years. He had a large family and a lot of *simchahs*, and he had me come to play at five affairs.

And then, the sixth time came. When he called, I noticed I wasn't feeling angry at him anymore, maybe because I'd already made him pay enough for what he'd done to me, or maybe because his compliments on my playing had mollified me somewhat. I don't know.

When he asked me how much I wanted this time, I started hemming and hawing: "Let me see...I have to think about this a bit..."

"You know," he interrupted, "I've noticed that you haven't ever raised your price since I first hired you."

Of course I hadn't raised my price. With other pleased clients, I would raise my price by fifty dollars or so, but with him, my price was grossly inflated in the first place. Something told me enough was enough, and I heard myself stammering, "Um, I'm going to offer you half price this time…two hundred and fifty dollars."

There was a moment's silence, and then he said, "Thank you for giving me such a nice discount. You know, I would have hired you at the full price, because my kids like your playing better than anyone else's."

He hung up, and only then did I realize that I'd completely gotten over my anger. It was amazing. I'm forty-six years old, and most of my life I'd hated this man. And now, all of a sudden… what a difference!

This time, the celebration was a bar mitzvah for one of his grandchildren. That night, I played like I'd never played in my life. I felt emotionally involved. I really wanted to make all those people happy.

At the end of the party, he came over and paid me, as usual, in cash — two hundred fifty dollars, as agreed. As he handed me the money, he said, "Thank you," and added very softly, "Avrumi."

I looked at him. It's been decades since anyone called me Avrumi. That's what they used to call me as a kid. He gazed at me, and I could see he recognized me — and not that he'd recognized me just now, but that he'd recognized me already from the first time he'd asked me to come to play at the *Sheva Berachos*.

"Avrumi," he said, "do you forgive me?"

I was completely stunned. A million thoughts ran through my head. Thoughts of awkwardness, of pain, of old memories, and a nagging question: Did he know that I had purposely overcharged him?

He didn't leave me wondering for long. "Everyone hurts others at times, but not everyone is privileged to become aware of the wrongs he has done in order to try and put things right. I heard from a mutual acquaintance that you were still angry at me and that you resented me terribly over that incident with the ruler. I realized that even if I asked for your forgiveness, you wouldn't be able to grant it wholeheartedly. So I hired you to play at my *simchah*s, to try and get close to you. I noticed your shock the first time I called you, and I realized that you were quoting a high price in order to drive me away. But I decided to go ahead anyway, because I felt that Hashem had given me the opportunity to go beyond asking forgiveness in order to somehow try to make it up to you.

"This time, when you told me you were giving me a lower price, I realized that you weren't hurting so much anymore, since you no longer felt the need to penalize me. So now I can ask you to forgive me. Believe me, I'm thoroughly ashamed of myself over what happened. And I'm truly sorry not only for the physical pain that I caused you, but for the emotional pain that you've suffered.

"I'm not a young man, and no one knows how long he's going to live. This has been weighing on my conscience. Don't ask me to explain why I did what I did, because I have no explanation. I must have been having a very hard day, although that doesn't justify my behavior. But I ask you to forgive me wholeheartedly, and when I've completed 120 years, I hope you'll come to my grave and tell me so."

I was touched to the depths of my soul, and I assured him I'd forgiven him already, even before he asked. He was moved to tears.

Tears came to my eyes, as well. I really did forgive him —

and with a whole heart. I felt like a heavy stone had rolled off my heart — a stone of anger, hatred and unpleasant memories. It taught me that when a person forgives an injury, he relieves himself of an awful burden.

Years passed, and a few months ago, this man passed away. There were a lot of people at his funeral, some of them relatives and some, former students. After the funeral, I looked at that mound of earth, and many thoughts passed through my mind. Thoughts about life, about the mistakes we make, and our ability and privilege to rectify them.

I thought about how the deceased had wronged me, and yet he had been wise enough to put things right during his lifetime. I can bear witness that I truly felt no anger towards him. The investment he was willing to make to atone for that wrong had touched my heart, and had healed the deep wounds that time, even decades, had not erased.

A person can repent even for an old injury to another, and if he'll only do it with enough sensitivity and wisdom, he can be completely forgiven.

I waited for all the people to leave, and when I was alone by the graveside, I said in a quiet voice that only he and I could hear, "I forgive you. You were a special person. I can really and truly say that I bear no ill feelings towards you. You appeased me, and you taught me how to appease others. May you come to the World of Truth purified and cleansed, and not be punished on my account."

And suddenly, I began to cry a torrent of purifying tears for the man I had once hated and resented so much, and who, in his wisdom and nobility, had succeeded in turning my hatred into love.

# A Short Visit with the Prime Minister

ere I am, writing to you once again. It's us, the Yerushalmi couple from Meah Shearim who goes to the Western Wall every day and reads the notes people push between the stones — that is, my wife reads them. I myself would never do such a thing!

However, this story isn't about the Western Wall; it's about Yitzchak Shamir when he was prime minister of Israel.

I bet you're wondering why I would be writing about Prime Minister Shamir.

Don't worry, you'll soon understand.

Don't think I have any connections with Yitzchak Shamir or with the government. I don't even vote in the elections, because in my neighborhood they don't look kindly on people who take part in the elections. So, I never vote... that is, except for the one or two times that I just couldn't hold back and I voted for Agudas Yisrael — only because the situation was critical, you understand.

My wife, on the other hand, always goes to the polls, and when I ask her who she votes for, she says it's against the law to tell. I know that she votes for Agudas Yisrael, and when I tell her that, she doesn't answer. But I can tell from the look on her face that I've guessed right.

Although, there was one time when I think she voted for a different party because its leader was involved in some kind of scandal in France and they wanted Israel to extradite him. He was trying to get elected to the Israeli Parliament so that he would have immunity. Sure enough, he was elected and wasn't handed over to them. As far as I was concerned, though, they could've given that thief to the French to face the music. But for my wife, it's a matter of principle never to hand a Jew over to the gentiles — even if he is a thief.

The story I want to tell you took place about twenty years ago. One day, our neighborhood mailman was fired. We loved our mailman. He was a nice fellow; and if he knew that a certain letter was urgent, he would even come to deliver it outside of his regular work hours.

But one day, he was fired. They said he'd destroyed a letter instead of delivering it.

The whole neighborhood was upset that he'd been fired, but there were some who said, "If he did something like that, then of course they had no choice but to fire him."

Whoever said that didn't know our mailman — either that, or he had no heart. We folks who knew him were very upset. I mulled it over quite a bit and decided that I had to take action.

So one morning after *davening* I say to my wife, "We're going out."

"Where?" she asks.

"To a certain place," I say. I don't say where, because if I do, I know she'll refuse to come.

She tries to get the secret out of me, but I hold my own, and after a while she gives in and agrees to come along. I know her; her curiosity always gets the better of her.

We go out to the street and I hail a cab. We get in, and I say to the driver, "Take us to the prime minister's house."

He looks at us once; he looks at us twice. He's about to ask what this is all about, when my wife does it for him. "What do you want with the prime minister?" she asks.

"Wait and you'll see," I answer, and I say to the driver, "You're going to the prime minister's house, on Aza Street or somewhere around there."

My wife catches the word "Aza" and gets scared. I explain to her that "Aza" is the place where the prime minister lives, and she asks, "Why does the prime minister live in Aza?" She thinks he lives in the Gaza Strip. I explain to her that he lives in Jerusalem, on a *street* called Aza, and not even on Aza Street exactly, but somewhere around there.

We arrive in front of the prime minister's house, and I say to the driver, "I'm just going in to tell him something; I'll be right back."

He gives me a pitying look and says to me, "If you manage to get in there, I'll take my hat off to you — and I'll also take you home for free."

"I'm not going in exactly," I explain. "I just want to exchange a few words with the prime minister."

"Mister," the driver laughs, "you're not going in, and you're not going to exchange even one word with the prime minister. If you even get to *see* the prime minister from six feet away and he hears you asking him something, I'll still take you home for free. And if you actually get to talk with him, I'm at your service for free for a whole month!"

"Remember you said that," I tell him.

"I'll remember," he answers.

And my wife tells him, half angry and half proud, "Apparently, you just don't know my husband."

      ✐      ✐      ✐

I walk up to the gate of the prime minister's house and knock on it. Two burly men promptly come up to me and say, "What do you want here?"

I tell them, "I want to talk with the prime minister."

They look at each other, and say to me, "Mister, are you looking for trouble?"

I try pushing on the gate, and just then, it opens and someone comes out. I say to my wife, "Come on, here's our chance to go up to the door."

But the two burly young fellows block our way, and they say, "Mister, you have no entry permit. This is the prime minister's house."

"I know it's the prime minister's house," I tell them. "If it were your house, believe me, I wouldn't have paid for a taxi to come here."

A few other very tall fellows with little earphones stuck in their ears come over, and one of them asks me, "Do you have an appointment?"

"What do I need an appointment for?" I say. "Do you think the prime minister has any reason to meet with me? I just want to give him an important message. I think he can help in the matter."

"Tell it to me," says the tallest one, who appears to be in charge.

"It's a private concern pertaining to us and the people of Meah Shearim," my wife tells him, "and we can't have outsiders interfering in the affair of the fired mailman."

My wife always reveals all the cards without even realizing it.

         🎬       🎬       🎬

His walkie-talkie beeps, and a voice asks, "What's going on?" The burly young fellow who's blocking our way says, "There are two people here from Meah Shearim who want to talk to Shamir. I was just about to send them on their way."

"Why should you send us on our way?" I ask. "You haven't even sent word to the prime minister that I want to talk to him."

There's a man looking on from the side. He looks like some sort of advisor. How can I tell? Because he's wearing a jacket that doesn't match his shirt, his tie or his trousers. He's staring at us, and when he sees that they're starting to push us, he says, "Just a moment. Let me hear what they have to say." I tell him briefly what we're there for, and he says, "Wait outside; I'll see if I can arrange something."

So we wait outside, and the guy with the different-colored clothes runs inside. The taxi driver uses his hands to ask us what's going on, and I signal to him that everything's under control.

A few minutes later, the gate opens, and the man with the mismatched clothes says, "Follow me."

"Thank you, my friend," I say coolly to the guard who gave us a hard time, and my wife gives him a sour "You see?" look, and we go up to the door of the house.

There, they ask to see identification. (In Israel everyone is issued ID cards.)

I don't have my ID card on me, and on second thought, I'm not sure I have one at all. I have no use for it. But my wife does, and her card says that I'm her husband, and that satisfies them. They conduct a quick search of her handbag, and they discover that my wife isn't carrying a weapon.

We go upstairs. The prime minister has a nice house, with lots of pictures. Someone ushers us into a waiting room. My wife remembers the taxi and starts fretting, and I say to her, "The driver probably left. He must have seen that he lost the bet."

And then they call us and say we can go inside. The prime minister looks very short. He's wearing a shirt without a tie, and he asks, "What brings you here, my friend?"

I say, "We came about the mailman in Meah Shearim who got fired. As prime minister, it's your duty to give him back his job."

He chuckles and says, "I'm not responsible for hiring and firing postmen, and if he was fired, there must have been a reason."

"Listen to the story I'm going to tell you," I say to him, "and then decide for yourself."

This mailman is already sixty years old. He's worked in Meah Shearim for thirty-five years, and his service has been out-standing.

On our street lives an elderly couple that was childless for many years. Forty years ago, when they were both forty-two years old, they had a son. They pampered and spoiled him — and he ended up going off the straight and narrow. First he started hanging out in the street, then he stopped putting on *tefillin*, and finally he took off his *yarmulke* and brought trouble and shame upon his parents.

Somehow he got mixed up with some shady characters. The next thing we knew, the police came looking for him. Someone had warned him about it, and somehow he managed to slip out of the country and run off to America. He would send his parents a postcard from time to time, telling them he was making a big success of himself there. According to his letters, he had repented of his evil ways and returned to the religion of his fathers. Not only that, he had opened up his own business. Although it was hard work, he wrote, he was becoming rich and successful.

Of course the parents were very proud of their boy for becoming religious again, and, although they missed him, they were glad they could count on him to carry on their family heritage.

They would show his letters to their friends, and the whole neighborhood would gather around to hear them read the latest report of their only son's great success.

No one ever asked why he never came to visit, why he didn't get married, and why he never sent any money.

And why didn't we ever ask? Because we knew the answer. The true answer, which they didn't know: Their son had never repented of his evil ways, and the only hard work he was doing was in the carpentry shop of the federal penitentiary in which he was imprisoned. We had heard that some time after he'd arrived on the golden shores of America, he'd committed some serious crimes. He was caught and sentenced to life imprisonment.

We were informed of these details by a Meah Shearim resident who traveled regularly to America and had inquired after the young man. There aren't any secrets in Meah Shearim, and we all knew his doings and his whereabouts, but we never dreamed of telling the truth to his poor parents, especially when those letters from him gave them the only speck of happiness in their bitter lives.

This went on for years. Whenever that fellow traveled to America, he would visit the couple's son and bring back a letter from the prison (in a plain envelope, of course). Sometimes he would bring them gifts, as well — all sorts of things the old couple needed: blankets, a room heater, a fan — telling the couple that their son had sent it from America.

✍    ✍    ✍

More years passed. The couple grew very old and what kept them going was the *nachas* they had from the knowledge that their only son was doing well in America. Of course, questions could have come up — questions like why he didn't come to visit once in a while.

But for some reason the couple didn't ask these difficult questions, except once when the old woman said to her friends, "It's a pity he's so busy that he can't come and see us, but what does a mother need more than to know that her son is so successful?"

One day, the woman passed away, and her last words were, "Tell my son I said thank you for the happiness he gave me in my life." The son "sent word" that he wouldn't be able to come for the funeral because of pressing business concerns — although his constant business at that time seemed to be starting fights in the prison yard and things of that sort.

The father continued receiving the letters, and they made him happy.

Time passed, and the father, too, became ill and his death was drawing near. That was when an official letter arrived from the federal authorities of the United States, to inform the parents that their son had been killed in a prisoners' brawl, and had been buried in the prison's cemetery.

Now, this letter reached the hands of our mailman, and as soon as he saw the return address on the envelope, he knew no good would come of it. So before he put it into the father's mailbox, he opened it and read it, and then took out his cigarette lighter and burned it, before it could reach the hands of the elderly father, who was then living out his final hours.

Just at that moment, a police car went by, and our mailman was arrested for destroying undelivered mail, an offense carrying a heavy penalty. The next day, the postal authority announced that he was fired.

✎      ✎      ✎

"That's the end of the story," I say to the prime minister. "My wife and I came here to tell it to you. If you believe the mailman's act was justified, then we'd like you to talk to the Minister of Postal Services and tell him to put the poor man back on the job."

As I finish my story, I feel tears on my face, and I try to wipe them away. To my surprise, I see that even the prime minister is blinking a little, even though everybody says he's such a tough guy. The fellow with the jacket and the trousers and the tie looks really touched.

The prime minister says to me, "There's no such thing as a Minister of Postal Services."

"Why not?" I ask. "Binyamin Mintz was Minister of Postal Services when I voted for Agudas Yisrael."

"Apparently the last time you voted was a long time ago," says the prime minister. "Today there isn't any Minister of Postal Services. There's a Minister of Communications, and I will instruct him to do something about this mailman of yours." Then he claps me on the shoulder and says, "You can go home now. You're a good Jew, and thank you for visiting me here."

"We've spent half a day on this," my wife says to him. "And they made trouble for us at the gate, too. They won't let you talk with anybody in this country. If I have to waste half my day every time I need to talk with the prime minister, how am I supposed to get my housework done?"

*36*

The prime minister smiles and gives me a look that says he's heard this kind of talk before — just like any other married man. I give him a wink, and we part in friendship.

We leave the prime minister's residence, and suddenly we see that the taxi driver is still waiting for us.

He was in shock over the fact that we were in there with the prime minister for half an hour. True to his word, he gave us a special telephone number to call his dispatcher and order free taxi service for a month. "Great," I say to my wife, "we can go to the Kosel by taxi."

The next day, our mailman was already seen making his rounds in our neighborhood, and telling everybody that his boss had come to him at night, after he'd gone to sleep, and told him that his dismissal had been canceled and that he should return to work. When he'd asked how this had happened, his boss said, "Don't ask. The prime minister intervened on your behalf."

Of course, the mailman thought this was an exaggeration and the boss was just pulling his leg. But on the other hand, the boss had shown him great respect by coming personally to his house.

That's the story, Rabbi Walder. If my children hadn't told me it was interesting, maybe I would have just forgotten about it. They think it's a big deal to talk with a prime minister. But I know the truth. It's easy. Just go to his house, knock on the gate, and state your business — but keep it short.

# Lost and Found

I read the story you wrote in the newspaper about the woman who'd lost a diamond ring and whose husband bought her another one, and I would like to tell you what happened to me. My story involves two different lost objects, and each has a lesson to teach.

I grew up in a very poor family. Actually, our finances — or lack thereof — were the least of our troubles. My parents were weak people, and both had emotional problems. They didn't get along with each other, much less with their children. My brothers had strayed from the path, and so there was no reason why I should choose a good path, either.

When I was younger, it wasn't so bad. I went to our local Bais Yaakov, and despite my family situation I managed to do well in school. The problems began after I graduated from the eighth grade.

I was accepted at a second-rate high school, and I started making undesirable friends. Some of those girls were in school with me, and some had already been expelled.

It went on that way until I was fifteen. At that time, I was making a little money by babysitting for our neighbors — a young couple with a baby. I was willing to work for cheap, and they trusted me to watch their little girl. While I was there I would wash the dishes and the floor, too, without even being asked to do it.

☙ ☙ ☙

One day, my mother said to me, "Tell me, where are the neighbor's rings?"

"What rings?" I asked.

"Don't embarrass us any more than necessary," was my mother's response. "Just tell me where they are, and the whole business will end quietly. Otherwise they're going to call the police."

"But I didn't take any rings."

My mother started yelling at me to tell the truth, and I answered back that I *was* telling the truth.

When she saw that yelling didn't help, she began pleading with me to admit my guilt and be done with it. But, of course, I continued to deny that I'd taken anything.

After that, the neighbors came over. They said that the rings had been on the table when they left the house, and when they came home, the rings were gone. Since I was in the house all that time, I was the only one who could have taken them.

They threatened to call the police if I didn't return the rings. But I refused to confess to stealing anything. By now, my mother believed me, because she saw how adamant I was.

The neighbors called the police.

☙ ☙ ☙

I couldn't believe what was happening. A policeman came to the house and began interrogating me. I told him that I had been in the house watching the baby, but I had absolutely not taken the rings — in fact, I hadn't even noticed them.

The policeman told my mother that he thought I was telling the truth, and since there was no evidence, the matter would be dropped. He told all this to the young couple, as well, and from that day on they no longer asked me to baby-sit for them. After all, who would want a thief in their house watching their daughter?

The episode had a terrible effect on me. I started going downhill in every way — in my studies, in my spiritual life, and in my emotional health. I knew I was the victim of an injustice, but I felt that nobody truly believed me. I didn't want to leave the house; I didn't want to see my friends.

After about a month of this, the neighbor came to my mother and told her she'd found the rings. She'd been out someplace that day and had taken them off. Now, a month later, she happened to return to that place and saw that someone had put up a notice saying that two rings had been found. The neighbor told my mother that she and her husband apologized, and they bought me a gift, a wallet, to try and make up for wrongfully accusing me.

My mother was overjoyed and brought me the wallet. As soon as I heard the story, I asked my mother, "Why don't they apologize to my face? They didn't hesitate to accuse me, and now that they see I'm innocent, they don't have the nerve to face me!"

In a rage, I threw the wallet out the window. I was absolutely livid. All the anger and pain I'd been holding inside for a month, I took out on that wallet. Today, when I think back, I still can't understand where they got the nerve to buy me a wallet — a wallet, of all things! But on second thought, no matter what they would have bought, I would have considered it chutzpah. I didn't need their gifts.

I was embittered over the injustice in this world, and I behaved accordingly.

❧        ❧        ❧

One day, while I was in the center of town, I noticed a fat wallet lying in the gutter next to the curb where I was standing. I bent down and picked it up, and walked around the corner into an alley to examine it more closely, away from prying eyes.

There was over two thousand dollars there, plus a check book and some credit cards.

I'd never seen, let alone held, that much money in my life. To tell you the truth, for a moment I was tempted to take it for myself, thinking that maybe the owner had given up hope of ever finding it. But then I remembered my obligation to return a lost object if it had identifying marks. I went home and I called the phone number that appeared on the checks. The address was in very upscale neighborhood.

A woman answered the phone, and I asked her if she'd lost something. Immediately she got all excited and said that she'd lost her wallet. She wasn't really worried about the money, she said, it was more the hassle of losing her driver's license and credit cards. I gave her my address and told her that if she wanted, she could come and pick up the wallet.

She arrived with her husband in a really fancy car. They looked like very wealthy people. My mother invited them in to the living room, and I went to get the wallet.

When I handed it to the lady I asked that she count the money, so that she would know that I hadn't taken any of it. She said she had no intention of counting it — that she trusted me. I insisted, and when she absolutely refused, I took the money and started counting it before her eyes.

She didn't understand why I was doing that, so my mother

told her the story of what had happened to me because of the neighbor's rings. My mother burst into tears, and I joined her. The rich couple also had tears in their eyes.

They gave me a large amount of money as a present, and they asked for our phone number.

From that day on, they became my guardian angels. They sent me money, and gift certificates to buy clothes. When they found out where I went to school, they used their connections to get me accepted into a really good school not too far away from our home. They even paid for me to have private music lessons.

The lady would come visit regularly and take me shopping with her. Every time we returned from such trips, I'd come home loaded down with goodies.

She was a psychologist, and she shared a lot of her knowledge with me. She helped me through my moments of crisis, and she strengthened me spiritually, as well.

I grew up as the princess of the family. I became mature and serious, well-dressed and well-spoken. My brothers and sisters saw how my life had turned around and followed in my footsteps.

When I was ready for *shidduchim*, the couple announced their intention to pay for everything. Their generosity knew no bounds; they gave me their heart and soul.

*Baruch Hashem*, a wonderful young man was suggested as a possible match — a *yeshivah bachur*, who was truly God fearing. It wasn't long before we became engaged. Again, my guardian angels stepped in and provided me with everything I would need to set up my new home.

Our wedding was the happiest day of my life.

Today I work as an accountant, and my husband teaches. We have seven children attending excellent schools. I am still closely in touch with my benefactors, and they've been supportive all the way.

Looking back, I never would've believed things would turn out so well.

I tell this whole story to my children, and I dwell especially on the part where I find the wallet. I say to them, "Human nature can be so blind. At that moment, I thought I'd found a treasure. If, God forbid, I hadn't withstood the trial, if I'd given in to the temptation to keep the money instead of fulfilling the mitzvah of returning a lost object, I would've been able to buy a lot of nice things. But that money would've been spent pretty quickly, and I would've lost something much greater.

"But I resisted the temptation. I did the mitzvah of *hashavas aveidah* and returned the wallet to its rightful owner. I gave up what was to me a small fortune, but I was granted endless good fortune. I received a wonderful life on a silver platter."

That's the story. I would've liked to tell you who my benefactors are, but I know their modesty and nobility of spirit. They wouldn't want their name to appear in print.

Instead, I'll mention only Hashem, the Creator of the world, Who saved me from falling into the trap of despair after I was falsely accused. And even more than that, He helped me pass the test when I found something that didn't belong to me.

# Pictures from Life

Y ou write stories and call them "stories from life." I have a story for you, Rabbi Walder, and I already have a title for it as well: "Pictures from Life."

Ask anybody what they would do if a fire broke out in their house. Which items would they try to save from the flames? A religious Jew would say, "First, I'd save my *tefillin*." But a lot of people would say, "Take the money and the photographs."

Photographs are precious to everyone. For many people, they're the only tangible record of their lives. In fact, I advise everyone to keep a series of pictures of every member of the family at various ages some place safe, like in a fire-proof safe, if possible. Material possessions damaged in a fire can be replaced, but not so the family pictures.

If you're wondering why I'm so interested in pictures, it's because photographs are my business. I own a photo shop in the middle of a busy shopping district — the kind of shop that has thousands of people coming in to develop their film.

My customers can be grouped in three categories. First, there are the one-time customers. They're passing by and

happen to have a roll of film on them that they've been meaning to develop or pictures that they want to have printed.
They notice a photo shop, so they bring in their film. They
come back an hour later to pick up their pictures, and I never
see them again.

The second category is made up of the customers who
come to you once in a while. You get to know them super-
ficially, and you learn things about them from their pictures.
The majority of my customers fall into this group.

Lastly, there are few customers who are true regulars and
come to you for all their photo needs. You may never exchange more than a few words with them, but through their
pictures, you know all about their lives. Some of these people
have been using the services of my store for twenty or thirty
years.

Sometimes you get some interesting surprises from the
customers in the first category, the one-timers. You might see
a picture of them with someone famous or on a fabulous trip
to someplace exotic, like India. It adds variety to your work.
Sometimes you might even be tempted to print another copy
for yourself — something I would never do, because the picture isn't my property.

The second type, you get to know a little better; but since
they don't come often, you forget what they brought in the
last time and you don't have continuity. It's like reading a
story that comes out as a serial, but with gaps of months or
even a year between chapters. You can't remember who's who
and you don't feel any bond with the central characters.

But with your regular customers, the ones who come in
often for many years, you get to feel like part of the family
— if only through their pictures.

My story is about people I came to know in that way.

It all began thirty-six years ago. My store was the only photo shop in the neighborhood. One day, a young man in his twenties came in and gave me a roll of film to develop.

I developed the film, and the pictures showed an average family. A young father (the man who had brought the film), a young mother, and two small children — about two and three years old. A picture from nursery school, a picture on the bus, a picture of them sitting on the grass. Completely standard.

The next day he came back, paid, looked through the pictures, and left.

The next time he came, there was a difference in the pictures. The mother and father were the same people, but they had other kids with them, the youngest looked to be about twelve, while the other two were further into their teens. The third time, the pictures showed the two of them with a pair of twins around fourteen years of age, and two girls of about nine and ten.

I was all confused. What was going on here? Were these people the parents of all these kids? Maybe they were older than they looked. But why would they have their picture taken with only a few of their children every time? I couldn't understand it.

Besides, each set of pictures seemed to be from a different place. And there was no family resemblance between the different groups of children.

As manager of a photo shop, with the thousands of pictures I see every week, I'd never seen anything like this. It was strange and intriguing.

A year passed, and the man came in again with a few rolls of film. I could see from the pictures that one of the boys had become bar mitzvah.

I decided to try and start a conversation. "*Mazel tov,*" I said. "I see you made a bar mitzvah for your son."

"He's not my son," said the customer. "Do I look old enough to have a thirteen-year-old son?" And he left.

It was true; he still looked like a man in his twenties, too young to be making bar mitzvahs. But I couldn't think of any explanation; the whole thing seemed so peculiar.

The next time he came in, I asked him frankly: "Tell me, what's going on in these pictures of yours?"

"Do you really want to know?" he said. "It's a long story."

"I've never been so curious in my life."

"Well, then," he said, "the story began when I was ten, and my father passed away. My mother had to raise us on her own. It wasn't easy, but she was very devoted and she managed it somehow. But then, when I was eighteen, the doctors found she had a serious illness.

"I was the oldest, and I dedicated myself to taking care of her. This went on for over two years. By that time she was very ill and she asked me to start looking into *shidduchim,* so that she might have the pleasure of seeing me married before it was too late.

"I did as she asked. I started looking for a *shidduch.* It was a little hard, because not too many girls want to marry a boy who has been orphaned of his father and would probably be orphaned of his mother, as well. But I did have a good reputation, and I found a *shidduch* — a fine girl from a good home, with two wonderful parents.

"My mother came to the wedding in a wheelchair, and everyone's eyes turned moist when they saw her. When I came over to the *mechitzah* to dance for her, there wasn't a dry eye in the hall.

"She passed on to the next world three weeks later.

"But I didn't have much time to wallow in my grief. I had four younger siblings: a pair of twin brothers, and two sisters. My wife and I had to take care of them, and I mean we had to supply all their needs: food, clothing, health care — everything. In three weeks, we went from being young singles to being a couple with the responsibilities usually reserved for middle age. I was already used to it, but it was hard for my wife. It's very much to her credit that she undertook the job without complaints.

"We had intended to buy our own place, but we moved in to my mother's home 'just for the meantime,' and took the place of parents to my brothers and sisters. 'The meantime' was a full year, and then another catastrophe occurred.

"My wife's parents were driving down the highway, when they were hit by a truck. Tragically, they were killed on the spot.

"The shock was indescribable. We were a couple of twenty-one-year-olds, facing disasters like these.

"My wife sat *shivah* with her siblings, while I stayed home to take care of 'our' children.

"Like me, my wife was the eldest, and she had three younger brothers. Suddenly we found ourselves with seven kids to take care of, four on my side, and three on hers. During the *shivah*, my wife gave birth to our first child, a boy. Now we had eight.

"Think for a moment, and imagine what was going on. I was twenty-one, still a kid myself, and I had to navigate between two houses full of orphans and visits to my wife and newborn son in the hospital. Neighbors and relatives were helping out, but as soon as my wife came home, we were on our own again.

"We sat down and did our homework. We had two properties and the life insurance from my wife's parents, plus a large amount in compensation from the accident. So we weren't short on money, but we didn't quite know how it should be divided up.

"We decided that everything should be shared equally, with no discrimination between the various sub-families. In other words, my wife's three brothers, my four siblings, and our own child would all get equal shares of the money.

"First, we pooled all our assets. We rented out my mother's house. My wife's brothers were old enough to stay at home if we were close by, so we bought an apartment in her family's building. That way we were there for her brothers, but not all thrown together in one house.

"This has been our living arrangement for four years now. As you saw, one of my wife's brothers celebrated his bar mitzvah in the meantime, and we have a little daughter of our own — our ninth child, in case you're still counting — and we're one big, happy family."

All the pictures I'd seen of the family flashed through my mind, and the pieces of the puzzle fell into place. Now I knew which ones were his siblings, which were her brothers, and which were their own children.

I began to follow further developments in the family with great interest.

Various trips and events took place, featuring the whole family together, with the happy young parents in the center, and it looked as though they had gotten used to living as a nuclear family unit.

Four years later, we come to the next stage of the story. One of the twins got engaged, and of course, I developed the pictures from the celebration. Sitting there together with the father of the bride, writing up the *tenayim*, the young surrogate father of the bridegroom looked more like a *chasan* with his future father-in-law. Then there were pictures taken during the engagement period, and of course, pictures from the *Sheva Berachos* dinners. (The wedding pictures I didn't see, since they'd hired a professional photographer for that event.)

Soon after that, there was another set of engagement pictures — the other twin.

More years passed and the couple's own little son celebrated his bar mitzvah, and the family pictures included two "daughters-in-law" and a few "grandchildren" taking part in the *simchah*, as well.

Another ten years down the road, the young man and his wife had five more children. By that time they had married off all the siblings under their care. Now it was time to start marrying off their own children.

🎬     🎬     🎬

About a month ago, thirty years after I first met that young father, he married off another daughter.

The couple is in their early fifties, and they have fourteen children, about seventy grandchildren, and believe or not, seven great-grandchildren. Of course, most of those "grandchildren" are actually their nieces and nephews, but considering how they raised and supported their siblings, they really are like devoted grandparents to all those kids.

When I heard about their daughter's engagement, I told the father to get ready, because I was preparing a very special gift for them. He didn't know what I meant, but I put days of work into that gift, and finally, the finished product was ready.

For the first time, I asked him to invite me to one of the *Sheva Berachos*, when the whole family would be there. He was surprised by my request, but he happily invited me to the last of the *Sheva Berachos.*

◿    ◿    ◿

The evening of the *Sheva Berachos* came. It was a lovely affair. A number of rabbis and family members gave very moving speeches.

When I was sure that the speeches were finished, I went over to the host and asked if I could say a few words.

He raised an eyebrow, but he said, "I'd be honored."

I quickly went into a side room where I'd left my best slide projector along with a big screen. Returning to the *simchah*, I set up the equipment and asked everyone to please turn their attention to the screen.

I turned on the background music I'd prepared, and began the slide show. It consisted of about 120 slides, starting from the third or fourth roll of film the young father had brought to my shop — that was when he'd first told me his story — showing the family history up to the present *simchah.*

First there was a picture of the young man and his wife with her sixteen-year-old brother, and then another picture with the ten- and eleven-year-olds. Bar mitzvah pictures, pictures from trips, pictures from engagement parties and pictures of their own newborns. Pictures of their "grandchildren," and more pictures of their own growing children. And then more bar mitzvahs, and pictures of a few genuine grandchildren — all in chronological order, all leading up to the present moment. Pictures that would show everyone — and especially the brave couple who were my acquaintances through pictures — just how long a road it had been and how proud they could be of their successful journey.

By the end of my little presentation, there wasn't a dry eye in the house.

The father of the family came over and hugged and kissed me, and his wife also thanked me with a great show of feeling. They said that never in their whole lives had they received such a meaningful and original gift.

That's the story, and now that I'm done, I feel that about ninety percent of it has been lost in the telling. How can I, in just a few pages, tell the story of thirty years of a family's life? It can't be done, but I've done the best I could as someone who has watched this saga unfold for thirty years, as someone who has carried this story in his heart all this time, and has to tell it before his heart bursts.

I've said very little about myself. You must be wondering who I am, other than the owner of a photo shop.

That's a story in itself. Maybe one day, Rabbi Walder, I'll sit down, write it all out and send it to you.

The fact is, I'm around the same age as the man whose life I documented in pictures. I have no children of my own, and probably never will. I've never even been married.

Somehow, though, I connected to this family through their pictures, and I see them as my own family.

I guess I'll never really be part of their lives — but I've got the general picture.

# The Cola Test

I'm a woman in my sixties and am now retired. I have a Russian woman who comes in a few times a week to help me with my housework. The truth is, my housekeeper came to this country without a work visa and she's terrified that if she gets caught they'll send her straight back to Russia. So she goes around disguised as a *chareidi* woman, with a wig and a long-sleeved dress. In our neighborhood, she fits right in.

I try to help her anyway I can; I've even offered to let her live in my house. My sons and daughters don't understand why I would want to go to such lengths to help her. They ask me why I don't want to hire a local woman, especially when this Russian cleaning-lady and I can hardly communicate with each other.

My answer to them is simple. Once you bring a local woman into your house to clean for you, she knows all your secrets within a week. Within a month she has basically seen everything that goes on in your house, and after a year, she knows your life better than you do.

How do I know that, you wonder?

Because I used to work as a cleaning lady.

🎬     🎬     🎬

I came to Eretz Yisrael in the 1950's, when there was a mass immigration after the establishment of the State of Israel. I was ten years old then. My family was very poor, and so I started cleaning houses to earn some money.

For those of you who don't know, in those days, all the household helpers were immigrant women and girls. We were very dedicated, and cleaned other people's houses as if they were our own. So people would hire us to do their house-work, and we did the work as it should be done, with all our hearts.

I worked for all sorts of ladies; believe me, I became a big expert on the different types. There were the mean ones who would treat you like dirt, and the nice ones who would treat you with respect. The nice ones would keep asking you if everything was all right, while some of the others wouldn't even know your last name. You were their cleaning lady; why should it ever occur to them that you had a family — or feel-ings, for that matter?

I worked for a lady who never even offered me a glass of water, and if it looked to her that the level of orange juice in the container had gone down by half an inch, she would ask, "Tell me, did you see who took some orange juice?" We both knew that nobody had been home but she and I, so the only person she could have been thinking of was me. She even had the nerve to add, "Not that I mind. I just wanted to know." Of course you just wanted to know, I would think to myself, although really I would've liked to tell her, "Don't worry, lady, I wouldn't even drink your water!" But of course that wouldn't be nice, now would it?

54

But other ladies would kindly offer me anything they had in their refrigerator, and always made sure to ask how all my relatives were doing, knowing each one by name.

Experience showed me that the ones who were nice to me were also nice to their husbands and their kids, and the mean ones were mean to everybody, including their own families. I hardly ever found one who was mean to the cleaning lady, but good to her family, or vice versa.

But getting back to the point, I always worked for at least two families at a time, and I knew all their little secrets. Don't think I'm the nosy type. I've always found people's lives interesting — but nosy? Not me.

However, to be a good cleaning lady, you need to keep your eyes open and be on the ball. For example, if you don't look at a bank statement, how can you know whether or not it belongs in the trash?

So, in the course of your work, you get a pretty good idea of the family's financial situation. You see the letters they get from the tax authorities. Things like that. There's no need to snoop; you can see it all from the papers they leave lying around.

Sometimes I wanted to give them some advice about how they should handle their finances, but it wasn't my place to say such things to my employer.

There was one time, though, that in passing I did say something, and I learned very quickly that it hadn't been a very good idea, because they jumped to the mistaken conclusion that I'd been rummaging through their papers. All of sudden the woman told me she was sorry, but they couldn't afford a cleaning lady anymore.

"Ma'am," I wanted to say to her, "you can most certainly

afford a cleaning lady." After all, I should know.

However, I was always careful and never talked about what I'd seen or heard. I had my professional ethics, after all.

It has always been my luck to work for at least one employer who was a lovely person, and another who was especially mean. The others were somewhere in between.

The story I wanted to tell is about two families at opposite ends of the spectrum.

Thirty years ago, I was working for a wonderful couple, whose children were the nicest, most well-mannered boys and girls you could ask for. I hardly had any work to do there, because they kept things so clean. All I had to do was tidy up a bit and dust, sweep and mop the floor — and of course, sort through any papers that had been left lying around.

They had a son, a delightful boy, gentle and considerate — a real *tzaddik*. I can testify to the fact that even when he was on vacation from yeshivah, he would get up early every day to *daven Shacharis* in shul. The only fight he had with his mother was when she complained that he was staying too long in the *beis midrash* and forgetting to come home for meals. Even on that point, he tried to be considerate, and sometimes he'd come home on time. When he was at home, he helped her all the time, and he treated her and his father with the greatest respect.

At the same time, I was also working for the Slobowitz family. That wasn't their real name, but it should give you an idea of the things they never exerted themselves to do — like picking up their junk, washing dishes, and sweeping the floor. After all, that's what cleaning ladies are for.

And what did they do the rest of the week, when I wasn't there?

# The Cola Test

They threw everything on the floor. Every room was littered with dirty laundry, and the kitchen sinks were full to the brim. Between Sundays and Thursdays when I would come in to clean, whenever one of them needed a cup, he would take one from the sink, give it a quick rinse, take a drink and put it back in the sink again. It never occurred to them that anyone besides the cleaning lady could wash a sinkful of dishes or run a mop over the kitchen floor.

The boys in that house were so lazy that they might not even have bothered to breathe if not for the fact that then they would die and could no longer be lazy. They would lie around the house all day, and when they wanted something, they would call out for someone to bring it to them. Of course, each one was lazier than the other, so if they wanted something, they would just have to pry themselves off the couch, or wherever they were sprawled out, and get it themselves.

But unlike the sons, who were just plain lazy, the family had a daughter who was something else entirely. Not only was she lazy, she was mean. Actually, I shouldn't say she was mean. She was really nasty.

She constantly showered her brothers with verbal abuse, and when I started working there she decided to make me her special project. She would follow me around, and if she felt that I'd missed a spot somewhere, she'd start ranting how they paid me good money for shoddy work.

I suffered in silence. I was careful not to give her an excuse to abuse me any more than she already did. Unfortunately, I really needed that job at the time. But in my heart I decided that I would quit working for them as soon as I could.

One day, when I arrived at their house for my biweekly cleaning, the daughter practically attacked me as soon as I walked in the door. "Today," she said to me, "you're to get things ship-shape around here. We want to see the job done right for a change."

I was insulted. "What do you mean, 'for a change?'" I said. "What's wrong with the way I clean?"

One of her brothers, who was lying on the couch, called out, "She has a *shidduch*-date tonight. This is their first date, so he's coming here, and my sister wants to make sure that the house will be really clean."

I started working, and everyone came to sit down and watch. They didn't help me clear the messy floors so I could wash them. Oh, no. They just sat there in a row like the Supreme Court and judged me. Not that I was expecting any kindness or respect from them. They sat there, talking and laughing, and every once in a while the girl would hurl some insulting remark my way.

Two days later, I went to clean the other family's house — the nice ones. The lady of the house asked me if I could do a little extra today, and make the place really sparkle. By way of explanation, she whispered in my ear that her son would be meeting a girl there that evening.

Naturally, I put my whole heart into it this time, and the lady and her daughter worked along with me. When everything was scrubbed and polished, we arranged the living room just so, and then I remembered that this was the second time this week I'd prepared someone's house for a *shidduch* meeting.

"So this is the first time they'll be meeting, is it?" I asked casually. My employer said, "No, the second. The first meeting is always at the girl's house."

I put two and two together, and I said to myself, "Oh, no! I hope it isn't *that* girl!"

I decided that I had to do something — at least I had

to find out if that wonderful boy was going out with Miss Slobowitz.

I took a long time finishing up the rest of the house. I even spilled a bucket of water "by accident" in order to stay a little longer.

Just as they opened the door to let the girl in, I was wringing out the mop in the bathroom. I opened the door just a crack, and who did I see coming in?

You guessed it! I couldn't believe that such a mean, abusive girl was dating the most refined, gentle boy I'd ever known, from the nicest family I'd ever met in my life!

What was I going to do?

Of course, I could go to the lady of the house and tell her what I knew, but I didn't know if that was the right thing to do. Besides which, I told you that it was my professional credo never to reveal things that I learned while working in other people's houses.

So I didn't say anything, and I went home feeling completely torn. I told my husband I had to do something, but I didn't know what to do.

"Go and tell the mother," he suggested.

"I haven't got the heart to do it," I said.

"So keep quiet, then, and let things take their course."

"I don't have the heart for that, either."

Somehow, the family had to find out who they were dealing with, but at the same time, I didn't want to be the one to tell them.

The next time I went to clean for the young man's family, I asked how the *shidduch* was going.

"Very well," said the boy's mother. "He'll be seeing her again the day after tomorrow."

"Oh," I said. "And where's the customary meeting place this time?"

"Now they can see each other outside the house. They'll meet in a hotel lobby."

"How nice," I said. "Which hotel?"

"The Hilton."

"Mmmm," I said. "An evening date?"

"Yes, we set it up for eight-thirty."

"I hope it turns out well," I said.

I went straight home and told my husband the latest developments. We sat down and racked our brains trying to come up with an idea as to what to do.

Finally, my husband, resourceful person that he is, came up with the perfect solution — Tzvi.

Tzvi is my husband's nephew and is a born actor. Give him a character to portray, and Tzvi will get right into it. Tell him to be a judge, and he'll sit there with his gavel, judging away. Tell him to be a taxi driver, and there you are, in the backseat of his cab.

So what did my husband want Tzvi to be this time?

A waiter.

Where? In the lobby of the Hilton hotel, of course.

At eight-thirty we were riding in a taxi, and Tzvi was with us. Tzvi knew his part well.

We saw the boy in front of the hotel, waiting for the girl. She arrived, and they went inside and sat down.

Tzvi sprang into action. Wearing what could pass for a hotel uniform, he slipped into the lobby, sidled over to their table and said, "May I take your order, sir?"

"What would you like?" the boy asked, turning to his date.

"Cola," she replied, and he told Tzvi to make that two colas, please.

With a slight bow, Tzvi backed off. He didn't put in their order at the bar, of course, since the hotel management didn't know of his existence. He came out to us. *We* were the bar. My husband ran to a nearby kiosk and bought two cokes.

I was prepared! I'd brought some nice glasses from the set we inherited from my mother-in-law, and a pair of white linen coasters. We set it all up on a tray, and Tzvi, balancing it expertly, sidled back in, placed the glasses in front of the couple, and proceeded to pour out cola — first for the young lady, and then for her date. It was time for Tzvi's *tour de force*. Turning suddenly clumsy, he spilled cola all over the table and it went dripping over the edge onto the carpet. The young couple jumped.

This was the moment of truth. We'd decided that if the girl reacted good-naturedly, then the boy was her prize. But if she did what I thought she would do, then he'd find out just who he was dealing with.

I don't want to tell tales, so I'll allow her to tell her own tale — and oh, boy, did she tell it. She shouted it for the entire world to hear. Apparently she'd completely forgotten about the date, and the impression she was supposed to have been making.

She let Tzvi have it! She told him she'd have his job, and his head, and his shoes and socks, too. Her date tried to calm her down, saying that it was just a little accident. The cola hadn't even spilled on them. But her fuse was already lit, and at that point no one could put it out.

Our work was done. We could go home now.

Tzvi didn't even need to be fired; he quit after only fifteen minutes on the job. He's good at that; he's often done it before.

The next day, I asked the boy's mother how the *shidduch* was going. "I don't know," she said unhappily. "My son says it doesn't look like such a good match after all."

Not such a good match? What an understatement!

*   *   *

That's my story. And what lesson does it teach? For one thing, I'm not going to give up my Russian cleaning-lady.

Here's a piece of advice for all you readers: Make sure your cleaning lady is a foreigner who doesn't speak the local language and isn't interested in any of your family affairs — not your finances, not your *shidduchim*, and not your shoe size.

And even better, make sure she doesn't care enough to waste a cola on you, and certainly not two colas. And one last thing — make sure she doesn't have a nephew named Tzvi.

# *Forgiven, Forgiven, Forgiven*

I 'd like to relate something that happened to us — to my husband, actually — a few years ago, because I think this story has a very strong message.

My husband has been in the teaching field for over thirty years. He has always been considered a successful educator who knows how to build a boy's self-esteem and bring out the best in him. He's not the fun, *chevreman* kind of teacher. He makes the boundaries clear and is careful to establish a certain distance between himself and his students, but at the same time, he isn't severe or overly strict. He has always been extremely dedicated, staying up late to prepare his lessons — something that I personally can attest to.

A few years ago, my husband started complaining of pains — sometimes in his head, sometimes in his stomach — and for the first time ever, he started missing days of teaching.

He went to a doctor who ran some blood tests. After all the tests came back normal, the doctor told him that he probably just needed to take few days off, to rest up. Call it woman's intuition, or maybe it's just that I know my husband so well, but I sensed that the illness wasn't physical. Something was bothering him emotionally.

I didn't tell him this in so many words, but I hinted that if he tried to ignore the pains and throw himself back into his work, I thought they might go away. This gave him the impression that I didn't care about his suffering, and I could tell that he was pretty insulted.

He was sure that sooner or later the doctors would discover what his problem was. He didn't even consider the possibility that he had a different type of ailment. However, it finally hit him in the face one day during one of his frequent doctor's visits, when the doctor said to him straight out, "There's nothing wrong with you physically. I think you need to see a psychologist."

That really broke him down. But instead of seeing a psychologist, he stayed at home, sunk in melancholy — or in plainer language, depression.

It's hard to describe the effect this has on a household.

A perfectly healthy man — even more than that, a man with leadership qualities — suddenly refuses to go anywhere and retreats into himself for no apparent reason. We weren't under any exceptional stress, aside from a few debts to pay after marrying off a couple of children. Other than that, everything was fine; so there seemed to be no explanation for my husband's depressed state of mind.

Things got so bad that he had to take an unpaid leave of absence from work, for an indefinite period of time.

The doctors put him on medication, but it didn't appear to help. Sometimes it seemed he was even more depressed. It was a terrible time for both of us.

At that point we turned to rabbis for help, asking for their *berachah*. We decided to approach one of the *gedolim* — a famous rabbi who was somewhat acquainted with our family. I had to overcome my feelings of shame to do it, but I went to this rabbi's wife, a great *tzadeikes* in her own right, and poured out the whole, sad story to her. I pleaded with her to speak to her husband about our problem and ask him to *daven* for us, and perhaps give us advice as to how to deal with the situation.

The next day, she called to give me the *rav*'s answer. The *rav* had said that my husband's condition could be the result of resentment that one of his students was harboring against him. He suggested that my husband try to figure out who might be bearing a grudge against him, so that he might ask that person's forgiveness. If he would be successful, there would be a good chance that the depression would pass.

I relayed to my husband what the *rav* had said.

It took him a few days to prepare himself mentally for the task. He was willing to do anything to regain his health, but he knew it would be difficult. He knew that as soon as he started asking around, word would spread and that might cause him tremendous embarrassment. Nevertheless, he decided that it was something that he must do.

What made the undertaking even more challenging was the number of students my husband had taught. He'd been teaching for thirty years. How was he going to track down over a thousand former students and ask every one of them to forgive him if he'd offended them in any way?

He decided to go through all the old class ledgers that he used to take attendance over the years. He would go through the lists of names and try to remember which students he'd had dealings with that might have caused them to harbor resentment.

He spent a week going through the ledgers. The mere act of recollecting all those memories caused him quite a bit of emotional upheaval, as he thought of these students from the past who were now grown men, raising families of their own. But he persevered and managed to divide the students into three categories: those he was sure had nothing against him, those whom he couldn't remember at all, and those who, judging from their grades and the comments he'd written down on their behavior, might have a grudge against him. He would begin by contacting students from the third category.

On the first day, he called five students. It wasn't easy to locate them all. He had to call their parents first and ask where their sons were living now and how he could get in touch with them. Finally he managed to reach them, and he told each one that he was asking for *mechilah*.

Most of them had enough sense not to ask why he was calling now, after all these years, but one of them said, "Why is the *rav* asking?" and my husband had to grope for some sort of answer. All five, however, said that they had nothing in particular against him, and nonetheless they were willing to say "*machul lach*" ("all is forgiven"), three times, as my husband asked. So far, so good. He had obtained formal forgiveness from five students.

The following day he moved on to the next few names in his roster. In the morning he would compile a list of phone numbers, and in the afternoon he would try calling.

This became his daily routine. Over the course of a few weeks, he contacted over two hundred of his students, and they all said they bore no grudge against him. Some of them said that, on the contrary, they had only good memories of him. All of them willingly granted my husband's request and recited the formula, "*machul lach, machul lach, machul lach.*"

Then, letters began to arrive. Letters from the students my husband had called.

First, it was just one letter, in which the writer told my husband that he hadn't said much on the phone because he'd been taken by surprise, but now that he'd had a chance to think about it, he felt he must tell him what a good teacher he'd been, how nice he'd been to him, and what a positive effect he'd had on his life. His praise was so effusive, it made my husband blush, and even I blushed when I read the letter. It certainly made us feel good, especially as it came during such a difficult time for us.

A few days later, two more letters arrived. They, too, were full of praise for my husband, and their writers took pains to inform him that he had no need to be asking them for forgiveness. They thanked him again for all that he had done for them.

From day to day, I could see the transformation in my husband's demeanor. Every time that a new letter arrived he would brighten considerably. He kept the letters in a loose-leaf binder and would read them over and over again — sometimes smiling, and sometimes shedding tears of joy. The letters and phone calls had a remarkable effect: My husband was coming back to life.

His functioning began to improve tremendously. He started going to the *beis midrash* to study, and the doctor was able to reduce his medication. I cautiously suggested that he end his sick leave and go back to work, but he wouldn't hear of it. I understood that he wasn't ready.

Over the course of six months, my husband managed to reach almost all his former students. There wasn't a single one who said he had any grudge against my husband, but they all forgave him just the same. My husband and I assumed that there must be a few among them who had held something against him, or who remembered afterwards that he'd wronged them in some way, but they were too polite to say so.

Meanwhile, the letters and phone calls continued streaming in, and my husband even formed new relationships with some of his old students.

One day, one of the students whom my husband had already contacted called back and wanted to speak with him. This man had been in his class over twenty years ago. Speaking in a low, hesitant tone, the former student said that although he had said in their last conversation that he bore no grudge against my husband, there was, in fact, something bothering him. Although he certainly forgave my husband for it, he thought it was important to let my husband know about it.

The former student did not want to speak about it over the phone. When my husband invited him to visit us in our home, the student said that he never left his house.

This was beginning to sound strange.

My husband asked for his address and told him that he would come the next day.

The address he gave indicated that he was living with his parents, meaning that apparently he'd never married, or perhaps he was divorced. We realized that the young man was seriously unhappy, but we didn't know just how unhappy.

My husband wanted me to accompany him, but I told him that I thought that maybe the fellow wouldn't appreciate my presence. So my husband called him back and explained that he would feel more comfortable if I were with him. The student said that he didn't mind, but that my husband might be embarrassed to have me there listening to the conversation. My husband replied that there were no secrets between us and that he would tell me everything that happened in any case.

To be honest, I was scared.

My husband looked into his class ledgers and noted that this student had been absent many days, but he couldn't remember why.

The next day, we went over to his house as planned. The young man's father opened the door for us. He told us in a whisper that his son had been in a deep depression for years and that he couldn't even remember the last time his son had agreed to see anyone other than a psychiatrist.

We both quickly made the connection between the young man's depression, the fact that he held something against my husband, and my husband's affliction.

The young man's father led us down a hallway and rapped on his son's door. My husband's former student was lying in bed, but sat up when we entered. His father introduced us and quietly left us alone.

It was a closed room. The windows were shut; there was a dank smell in the air. Everywhere was disorder, dust, and depression.

The young man began by asking how things were going at the Talmud Torah, but my husband stopped him by saying he had taken a leave of absence. The student asked why, and my husband didn't know what to say; he mumbled something about being a little unwell and fatigued.

Then, getting to the point, my husband said, "We came here to hear what it is that you've been holding against me all these years."

Speaking slowly and in a low tone, the young man said that as far back as he could remember, he'd had emotional problems. He was very intelligent, but his emotional makeup had never been strong. He'd had many ups and downs, and his teachers had taken him to task for his many absences.

In my husband's class, he said, he'd received better treatment. My husband had shown more understanding than the others; he was the only teacher who didn't get angry at him every time he missed class. He would simply ask him why he hadn't come to school, he would mumble that he'd been sick, and that was the end of it.

We still didn't understand what my husband had done wrong.

"For years," the young man went on, "you were the teacher I had the most pleasant memories of. You were the one who really understood me and sympathized with my suffering. Until the day you called me on the phone, if anyone were to ask me to list five great men, you would have been one of them.

"But when you called and asked me if I held anything against you, I realized there had to be something behind it. A man doesn't call up his old students out of the blue for no reason. I realized that you were probably in a bad state of mind. Of course I said I forgave you, but your phone call got me thinking, and I came to the conclusion that even if I didn't hold anything against you, I ought to."

I looked over at my husband and saw that he appeared as perplexed as I was.

"Let me explain," the student continued. "The other teachers were always getting angry at me for being absent, and at the time I thought that they were being mean to me. But I realize now that they were actually helping me, because they forced me to stay involved.

"You, on the other hand, were nice to me. I know you did it out of kind-heartedness, and maybe out of sensitivity, but

70

you let me get away with too much. Sometimes I'd be absent for over a week, and you wouldn't say anything. I think that the year I had you for my teacher I was absent more days than I came to school. Not only did you not get tough with me, you even argued with my parents because they were trying to force me to get out of bed and go to school.

"I remember one day when they just threw me out of the house, and you, being so kind-hearted, took me back home. You spoke to my parents at length, trying to convince them not to be hard on me, not to break my heart. They listened to you. They let me sink lower and lower. It was you who opened the escape hatch for me and allowed me to avoid responsibility.

"I can't blame you, because I know you meant well, but I thought I'd better tell you about it, because if you're asking for *mechilah* because you think someone bears a grudge against you, it could be that this is it.

"I don't think it's your fault that I ended up like this, but maybe if people had acted to prevent me from sinking, it wouldn't have happened. As soon as one person let me have things my way, the opportunity was taken away from other people who might have saved me.

"It's possible that deep down I was holding it against you after all. So now the time has come to bring it out into the open, and to forgive."

My husband and I were stunned. Suddenly, all the pieces fit together.

Now we understood why this melancholy had descended upon us, rather than some other illness. We understood why the *rav* had instructed my husband to ask for forgiveness, and we also understood something about the power that can be wielded, even unknowingly, by a person who bears a grudge towards another.

My husband started talking freely now, telling the young man unabashedly about the mental state he'd been in, about how he'd deteriorated and lost his whole world in a single year. We both cried as he talked. Finally, my husband sat down next to his student and said, "Please forgive me for not doing enough to help you. Please forgive me."

The young man said, "I forgave you already before you came here, and now I'll forgive you again." And three times he said "*machul lach.*"

We went home in silence.

The next morning, the first thing I said to my husband was, "You're going to call the Talmud Torah right away and arrange to go back to work."

He looked at me in amazement; I sounded so tough.

"I don't want you to hold it against me some day that I didn't push you enough," I told him. "So I'm going to do whatever I have to do to get you to go back to your work, to your life. And I don't advise you to put me to the test."

He looked at me, saw the sternness in my face — and gave in right away. He picked up the phone, called the school, and arranged to start work again at the beginning of the next month, which was two weeks away. During those weeks, he changed his mind many times, but I wouldn't let him get away with it. When the big day finally arrived, he went back to work and hasn't missed a day since.

We both took it upon ourselves to help his former student, and we actually took him into our own home. Slowly he

72

began to make progress. On the advice of his psychiatrist, he began going out to do volunteer work for one of the local *chesed* organizations. That was a difficult hurdle for him, and it took a lot of cajoling on our part before he agreed.

I must mention before I close, that my husband is still teaching, even though he's officially past retirement age. So I guess you could say that this story has a happy ending.

I wanted to tell you our story because of the important lessons to be learned from it. To all you teachers out there: Be careful with your students; you should not be unnecessarily harsh with them, but, as our story proves, it's not good to be excessively soft-hearted, either.

The second lesson applies to everyone: Even if you've been wronged by someone, try to forgive him in your heart. Bearing a grudge against another person can have devastating effects.

# Finding My Father

**M**y story is all about secrets and deception. Eventually, though, the truth came out. It was a long time in coming, but better late than never.

In my earliest years, I thought I had only one parent, since my mother was the only one around. It was when I was about five years old that I realized I was missing something. I would see other girl's fathers coming to pick up their daughters in my kindergarten class. Naturally, I asked my mother why I didn't have a father like the other girls. Her reply was a tight-lipped, "Because you don't."

The next time I brought up the subject, she told me never to ask that question again.

It took me another five years to get up the courage to ask again, and then was I really persistent. I would cry and carry on, and demand to know why all my friends had a father and I didn't. Finally, my mother told me that my father hadn't wanted me and had run away.

Well, you can imagine how much that bolstered my self-esteem. Everyone else had a father, because their fathers wanted them. I didn't have one, because mine rejected me. It wouldn't have been quite so bad if I'd had any reason to think my mother wanted me, but she was not the type of person to show affection.

She was an unhappy woman, poor and barely scraping by. She'd had a few jobs here and there, but for the most part she was unemployed. She didn't get along well with her parents, and often they wouldn't even be on speaking terms. She didn't have any type of relationship with her siblings — except for one sister. In fact, she quarreled with practically everybody — with neighbors, with my teachers, with the grocery man....

I don't know how I managed to turn out normal. I think there were two main factors. First of all, we had a very nice family in our building that used to invite me to come in and play with their daughters. That gave me a taste of what normal family-life was like, with a father and mother who got along. The second thing that I had going for me was that I did well in school. Hashem, in His goodness, blessed me with good learning skills and a nice appearance, which made me popular with my classmates, and that gave me the strength to keep going and growing.

Starting from about age twelve, I learned how to keep my home life — which was awful — separate from my school life — which was basically rewarding.

I think it was when I was about fifteen that I reversed roles with my mother. I'd become a mature teenager, and she stayed where she was. There was a lot of fighting between us at first, and then I figured out that the only way to keep from getting hurt was to surrender unconditionally. Once I'd done that, she calmed down and even started becoming dependent on me. She would cry on my shoulder and bemoan her fate, and I would try to comfort her, although I didn't really know how.

Once in a while, I would again ask her about my father. She'd always answer me sharply, saying there was nothing to talk about.

Many years have passed since then, and looking back on it, I have trouble understanding why I wasn't more persistent about finding out who my father was and why he had disappeared.

When I was nineteen, I tried asking my aunt if she knew anything about my father. She gave me a funny look and said, "Didn't your mother tell you?"

I said she hadn't. Unfortunately, I added that my mother had told me he hadn't wanted me and had run away. That was a mistake, because it ruined any chance I had of getting additional information from my aunt. Once she understood that this was what my mother wanted me to believe, she indicated that this was pretty much all she knew, as well.

When I was twenty, I got married to a fine young man. Since we had no money, our friends and acquaintances raised a sufficient sum to make a modest wedding, and I became part of a warm, loving family.

The wedding itself was an event I'd prefer to forget. From the day I got engaged, my mother started making things difficult, quarreling with my future in-laws, which hurt both me and my fiancé. I guess it was hard for her to let me go, and she was doing everything she could to break off the *shidduch*.

The wedding date drew near, and it was time to make up the guest list and address the invitations. She started vetoing a lot of the people I wanted to invite, including the only one of her sisters who was still on speaking terms with her. I insisted on inviting my aunt, as she was the only other relative I would have at my wedding. I couldn't believe that my mother would not want her own sister to come — especially when my aunt had so graciously offered to pay for part of the expenses. I tried to coax my mother out of her unreasonableness, but she was completely obstinate. "It's either me or her," she said.

A series of events ensued that I don't even want to remember. The worst was when the management of the wedding hall received a mysterious phone call saying that the wedding had been canceled. They contacted my *chasan*'s family, who in turn contacted me. We called the wedding hall back and told them somebody had been pulling a prank at our expense. My *chasan* couldn't understand who would want to play such a nasty practical joke, but I knew very well who the anonymous caller had been.

After that I didn't say a word to my mother concerning the preparations, so she wouldn't be able to spoil my plans.

I spoke to the manager of the hall, the photographers, the printer, and the florist, and I told them all not to take orders or pay attention to messages from anyone else.

"What if your mother calls?" one of them even asked. "Do you want us not to pay attention to her, either?"

"That's right," I answered. "Not even to her. No one can make changes but me."

You can imagine what it was like for me, a young *kallah* forced to arrange everything on her own, without a father or a supportive mother.

A few days before the wedding, my mother informed me that she wouldn't be coming. I can hardly describe how nervous and upset I was at the thought that she wouldn't show up — although deep in my heart I hoped she really would stay away. At the same time, I couldn't bear the suspense.

Well, in the end, she didn't show up, and I got married with no parent there, just my aunt and uncle, who led me to the *chuppah*. I was a pitiful bride, exhausted and dejected, knowing I was heading not just to my *chuppah*, but to my whole life, with nothing behind me but broken shards.

Although I was losing the only semblance of a mother I'd ever known, I was gaining a wonderful husband, a man of fine character, and a couple of wonderful parents, too — my in-laws, who treated me like their own daughter.

About a year later, our first son was born. Emotionally, it was a pivotal event for me. Suddenly, I felt my father's absence keenly. I don't know why, but having become a parent myself, something inside me snapped and I decided that I had to make every effort to find my father.

It was no use going to my mother for information. She had cut off all contact with me and moved away — thus disappearing completely from my life.

I decided that I would have to do the detective work myself. We live in Eretz Yisrael and so I assumed that my parents must have gotten married somewhere in Israel.

My husband understood my intense desire to find out more about my father, so he decided to go to the Ministry of the Interior to see if he could find out any information from the population registry. After explaining the situation, a very sympathetic clerk checked the computer database, but did not find any record of someone having been married to my mother.

I appealed once again to my aunt — this time insisting that she tell me everything. She finally relented and told me that my father wasn't from Israel. According to my aunt, my parents had been married in accordance with Jewish law, but they had never registered as a married couple with the Israeli government. Apparently, immediately after the wedding they began having problems getting along, and they divorced a month after I was born. She couldn't tell me anything more about my father — all she knew was his name and that he was from America.

We made some attempts to track him down, but his name is a common one, and it was like looking for a needle in a haystack.

It was very frustrating. I knew that my mother had the information I needed, and she was hiding it from me. I also knew that if I asked her, she'd refuse to give it to me.

Somehow I endured it for another few years. In the meantime, I had two more children, a girl and another boy; and with the birth of each one, came an emotional crisis, a powerful longing to discover my paternal roots.

✐   ✐   ✐

One day, I received an urgent phone call from a hospital. My mother had been in an accident, and the only name she had uttered was mine. I rushed straight there. My mother was in bad shape; she'd been hit by a bus.

I sat down at her bedside. She was trying to tell me something, but I couldn't make out what she was saying. After a while, the doctor came in and told me that my mother had sustained serious internal injuries. They had done everything possible, but he wanted me to be prepared for the worst.

I debated with myself: *Should I ask her about my father, or was that too improper a thing to do at a time like this?* I opted for impropriety and told her, "Imma, I want to know who my father is."

She said his name, the name I'd already heard from my aunt. I asked where he lived. She said somewhere in America, but she had no idea where he was now. I asked who his parents were, and where they lived. "It's all in the documents," she murmured. "It's all in the documents." She then closed her eyes, and a few minutes later she was gone.

I sat and cried for a while. Although we had become estranged, I couldn't believe that my mother was really gone.

At the same time it occurred to me that I might yet find out who my father was. All of sudden, I realized that I didn't even know my mother's address. How would I find the documents she'd mentioned?

Just then a nurse came in, carrying a handbag. "This belonged to your mother," she said, in a sympathetic tone of voice.

My husband made the funeral arrangements quickly. A handful of people showed up, mostly from my husband's family, but my aunt and uncle were also there. I sat *shivah* in my house, together with my aunt.

After I got up from sitting *shivah*, I decided that it was high time that I solve the mystery that had been tormenting me all my life. I went through the contents of my departed mother's handbag. Among them was a letter indicating her most recent address. Her keys were there, too. I asked my husband to go there and make a thorough search. He returned with an envelope stuffed with documents and pictures.

For the first time, I saw a picture of my father. There were documents giving details about him and his family, as well. I managed to find his parents' telephone number and didn't hesitate to pick up the phone and call them right then and there. I only hoped that it was still their number, since the information I had was from so many years ago.

Unbelievably, my father's mother picked up the phone. When I explained who I was, she became very excited. She told me that my father would be thrilled to hear from me. According to her, he'd been trying to locate me for years.

She gave me his phone number, but said that she would contact him first to give him the good news. She asked for my number so that she could contact me just as soon as she spoke with him.

A short while later the phone rang, and on the line I heard a deep, clear voice — my father's voice.

He said that ever since my mother had run off with me, he'd been looking for me without success. They'd been living in the States, he explained, and the divorce had been settled amicably, with visiting rights for him, child-support arrangements, and so on. But the first time he'd come to see me, he'd found nobody there. My mother had run away with me. Her parents wouldn't tell him anything, and her siblings didn't know where she'd gone.

He tried to track me down and eventually discovered that she'd gone back to Israel with me and had appealed to the court to issue a restraining order against him, claiming that he wanted to kidnap me.

Initially, he had wanted to fight it, but on the advice of his rabbis he dropped the matter and started focusing on finding a new wife instead. It wasn't long before he was engaged and then married again.

The story didn't end there. He and his new wife had expected to raise a family. Despite medical intervention, they remained childless. Eventually it became clear that they would never have children together.

My father thought of coming to Israel to look for me, but he knew it would involve legal entanglements and a difficult struggle. His wife told him she didn't like the idea, and again, reluctantly, he let the matter drop.

I couldn't believe what I was hearing. I had actually been born in the United States. It never occurred to me that my mother had ever stepped foot out of Eretz Yisrael.

The most important detail, though, was the fact that my father had really wanted me all along.

Then I got another big shock. My father told me that just this year, his wife had changed her mind, realizing that I would be an adult by now. She told him that he ought to try and find me. So together they traveled to Israel to look for me, but until that moment had been unsuccessful.

They were in the middle of packing their bags to go home when his parents called, telling him the wonderful news that they'd heard from me.

"You mean, you're here in Israel?" I asked excitedly.

It turned out that they were in a hotel which was only a ten-minute drive from our house.

"Please come right away!" I said.

Twenty minutes later, they were at our front door. My husband and I were sitting there waiting when the doorbell rang. My husband ran to answer it, and suddenly, my father burst into my life.

It had all happened so quickly, I can hardly describe it. All my life I'd wondered about my father, longed for him, and looked for him; and now, half an hour after I'd contacted his parents, he was standing before me. I just didn't know how to react.

I started by telling him how I'd reached his parents, that I had just got up from sitting *shivah* for my mother. He bowed his head sadly at that news, and after a moment he said,

"You are my daughter, and for twenty-six years I've been prevented from seeing you. Now I'm asking you to come back to me and let me be a father to you at last. I'm willing to live in Israel and be a grandfather to your children — the grandchildren I haven't seen yet." He voice cracked, and he started to cry. I cried along with him.

My father and his wife made *aliyah* shortly thereafter, and have since become full-time grandparents to my children. I get along fine with my stepmother; she sees me as her own daughter. They're very well-off, and they shower us with generosity.

I had nothing, and suddenly I have everything. We were a poor young family, barely managing to pay the rent, and suddenly, in a week, we had an apartment of our own (my mother's apartment, which I inherited). In that same week, I was reunited with my father. He's a wonderful, supportive person. Not only does he provide emotional and financial support, but most important of all, he gives me what I lacked all my life — a father image to look up to.

Yes, I got my father back. But I know that it has been my Father in Heaven, Who has been with me all along, carrying me past all the obstacles, never forsaking me when I was fatherless and virtually motherless, and never letting me fall into despair.

I hope this story will be a source of encouragement for others who have family problems. One or both of your parents may be missing or lacking in some way, but there is always a Father looking out for us, as it says in *Tehillim*: "Though my father and mother have abandoned me, Hashem will gather me in."

# *Tough Love*

R ecently, I read a story in one of your children's books. Although I'm far from being a child, when I read this story to one of my own children, it took me back to an episode from the past.

As a boy, I was well-liked. In *yeshivah ketanah*, I was very popular and was always surrounded by friends — more friends than I really wanted. Sometimes, they would even fight over the privilege of sitting near me in the *beis midrash* or the dining hall. I can't deny that I was flattered by it, but I never could understand why they would want to humble themselves like that before another person.

Those years in *yeshivah ketanah* passed quickly and easily, and then I went on to *yeshivah gedolah*. It was a large, well-known yeshivah, a whole new experience for me. Up until then, my standing in yeshivah had been secure; now, I had to make a new start.

I didn't realize that no one was rolling out the red carpet for me, or sounding the trumpets to announce my arrival. I strutted around the place like a peacock, expecting crowds of *bachurim* to come over and pull at my sleeves, begging me to be their *chavrusa*, their learning partner. But it didn't happen. No one ran after me. At first I thought they were playing ego games with me, trying to get me to come to them. Well, I was better at those games than anyone. I bided my time, waiting for them to give in.

My strategy failed. In the end, everybody had found a *chavrusa* except me and a handful of other boys. The problem was that those boys might have known how to open a Gemara, but there was no guarantee they would open it from the right end. I don't really mean that, of course, but I purposely wrote it here to show you what a superior attitude I had in those days, looking down on all my peers.

So I sat and learned by myself, and eventually I did find a *chavrusa* from another class.

I also didn't like my roommates and, of course, they returned my affection. I didn't try to make friends with the other boys, because I was used to being sought after by others. It took me about six months to realize I was in trouble.

All around me was a thriving social structure, groups of *bachurim* who enjoyed learning together and discussing problems over lunch or out in the courtyard.

And me? I was nobody. I wasn't even sure they knew my name.

I decided to make waves, to draw attention to myself. And that's when my real troubles began. I started mixing in to disagreements between some of the older *bachurim*, sticking my nose into everybody's business, and shooting off my mouth on every topic. Well, pretty soon everyone knew my name, all right, but they weren't exactly praising me.

I was known as an upstart and as someone who interferes

in things that are none of his business. At first I was in shock. I tried to fight it. I used my big mouth to defend myself, but I soon discovered that there were others with mouths just as big, and tongues just as sharp as mine.

I discovered something else, too; something I hadn't realized about myself. I discovered how vulnerable I was. I couldn't take it when people spoke against me or insulted me. When this happened, I'd be cut to the quick. I'd fly into a rage, which only served to further lower their opinion of me.

I didn't know how to handle my situation. I'd always been treated like a prince, and now I was being subjected to criticism and derision.

✒️    ✒️    ✒️

Then salvation came in the form of a new roommate — a sensitive, pleasant fellow who had never been involved in frictions. He made friends with me, and he enjoyed hearing my opinions. I was on Cloud Nine. At last, I had a real friend.

I made every effort to keep the friendship going. I asked him to be my *chavrusa*, and I arranged for him to be next to me during *davening* and meals, as well. Between learning sessions, we'd go for a walk or sit around and talk. I invited him to my house for Shabbos, and invited myself to his house.

I was proud of him in the same way that a person is proud of a new car. He was my prized possession, and with him, I felt strong and shielded from harm.

One day, when I saw him talking with one of the other *bachurim*, I suddenly felt a pang of jealousy.

When he finished, I went straight up to him. "What were you two talking about just now?" I asked.

"He asked me what time it was," my friend replied.

"Come on, don't fool around. What were you talking about?"

"I told you. He asked me what time it was and I answered him."

"Are you sure?"

"What's the matter with you, anyway?" he said.

He was right; something was the matter with me. From that day on, I started watching closely to see if anyone was talking to him, or Heaven forbid, getting *friendly* with him. He was *my* friend.

At first, I think he was a bit flattered by all my attention. But after a while it became clear that he didn't like being given the third degree whenever he had a conversation with someone else. Pretty soon he just got sick of it and started trying to fend me off by teasing me.

"What were you talking about?" I'd ask.

"I can't tell you. It's a secret."

"But you can tell *me*, can't you?"

"No, I can't. I promised him I wouldn't tell anyone."

"Not *even* me?"

"Not *even* you."

After that conversation, we stopped speaking. To be more accurate, I stopped speaking with him. I kept it up for an hour or two, and then I stood right in front of him, hoping he would ask me why I wasn't talking to him, but he pretended not to notice me. Finally, I asked him, "Haven't you noticed I'm not talking to you?"

"No, I didn't notice," he said.

He sounded so calm, it drove me crazy. "Then I want you to know that I'm not speaking with you," I announced.

"All right," he replied. "If that's the way you want it, no problem."

"What's with you?" I burst out. "Why are you torturing me

like this? And then, to top it all off, you make fun of me!"

"I'm making fun of you?"

"Yes. I tell you I'm not speaking with you, and you don't even ask why!"

"Okay. Why?"

"Because you're keeping secrets from me."

"Have you ever asked me not to pass on things that you've told me?"

"Are you equating me with him?"

"I'm equating one promise with another promise."

His apathy goaded me into chasing after him, quarreling with him, and then apologizing for it.

I started buying him expensive gifts, and then feeling bitter because he wasn't as loyal to me as I was to him. I told him not to talk to certain *bachurim*, and then I got mad at him for talking to them. In short, I tried to control his whole life, but the truth was it was I who was controlled by my abnormal dependence on him.

There were days when he would distance himself from me. I would notice it immediately. At first, I'd threaten him, then I'd try reasoning with him, and in the end I'd plead with him not to abandon me.

For him, it was confusing. On the one hand, he was flattered by my extreme attachment. On the other hand, he was scared by the intensity of my feelings. On the third, fourth, and fifth hands, he was getting sick and tired of it.

The next part is so embarrassing. I wish I could skip it, but it's too important to leave out.

I had been absent from yeshivah for a few days. When I came back, the boys asked me why I hadn't been around. I didn't answer them. But privately I told my friend, in the strictest secrecy, that I'd been diagnosed with a terrible form of cancer.

Of course, he was very upset to hear it, and he started bending over backwards to be nice to me. He apologized for all the times he made me feel bad, and promised always to be there for me from now on. For me, it felt wonderful. He was trying so hard not to hurt me. He would refrain from talking to the other *bachurim* and instead gave me all his attention.

We would even *daven* together for my recovery.

The only trouble with this arrangement was that it couldn't last. Not because I was dying of cancer, but because I wasn't.

It wasn't long before my friend's mother called my parents, all worried and concerned, to find out how much hope there was for me. My parents were surprised, to say the least, and told her that as far as they knew I was perfectly healthy. Within minutes, this conversation was reported to my friend.

He came to me and said, "Your parents claim you aren't sick."

I stared at him in a daze. "You spoke with my parents?"

"I didn't, my mother did. She called to ask them how you were doing, and that's what they told her."

My brain was working feverishly, looking for a way out. "I wish she hadn't done that," I said sadly. "My parents don't know. I don't want to cause them pain, so I'm hiding it from them."

He looked at me intently. I could see the disbelief in his eyes. He turned around abruptly and walked out of the room.

Here's what happened next: His mother called my parents again and told them my version of the story. Again, they assured her I was perfectly healthy, and said I must have been making up stories. Then my parents came straight to the yeshivah and gave me a tough talking-to. They called my friend's mother and made me get on the phone and admit to her that I hadn't been diagnosed with cancer or anything else. My friend was summoned home urgently, and came back with strict instructions from his parents not to exchange a single word with me.

This was a time of real crisis for me. My parents' anger gave way to pity. My father said, "You really are sick, but not with anything physical."

Those words pierced my heart. Suddenly I realized how low I'd sunk with this dependency of mine, and I was deeply ashamed. I felt completely worthless.

But if I thought my shame at being discovered would put an end to my dependency on my friend, I was wrong. After a while, those feelings of shame lost their edge, and I began trying to get close to him again.

First, I wrote him letters of apology. I received no reply. I tried pleading with him to talk to me, but it was like talking to a wall. I sent more letters; they came back unopened. Another *bachur* came to me to deliver an unequivocal message from my former friend: "Stay away from me, or I'll call the police."

It was the word "police" that brought me back to my senses. It made me realize how crazy I was acting. I was totally devastated. I didn't know how I could go on living without him. But it was only after I understood clearly that we would never be friends again that I starting rebuilding my life.

I transferred to another yeshivah and made a new start. I purposely tried to remain inconspicuous. I just sat and learned as if I wasn't particularly concerned with social success.

Little by little, *bachurim* began to approach me, wanting

to get acquainted. I didn't allow myself to get too excited about it, but I wasn't arrogant as I'd been in the past. I just took things slowly and moderately.

As one who'd been burned, I was extra careful. I realized that I couldn't allow myself to get too close to anyone at that point, because I knew my emotions were out of balance and I had a tendency to become overly dependent on others. So I limited my relations with others to the intellectual realm. This helped me not to fall into that trap again — not to put my well-being into another person's hands, not to crush my individuality, and not to make unreasonable demands of others. To allow them the freedom to talk to, or take a walk with, whomever they pleased.

I went to speak with someone about my problem, and he explained to me how the mechanism of dependency works. He said that when a person makes himself dependent on someone else, his personality gradually becomes more and more blurred. He taught me how to spot the feelings I had to be careful of, to recognize that moment when I wanted to surrender myself to another and make him the supreme arbiter of my self-worth. I had to be in control of my own life, he stressed, and not hand the reins over to anyone else. And at the same time, I must never even think of trying to control another — not his thoughts nor his actions.

I began to change. It's actually not so hard, once you acknowledge the problem and commit yourself to follow the rules. I went back to being what I had once been: an independent young man with a mind of my own. I didn't discuss my dependency problem with anyone besides my mentor, and it remained my secret.

Meanwhile, people in my new yeshivah saw me as an interesting person to talk to, and little by little, I became one of the most popular *bachurim* there.

When I came of age, I was offered some excellent *shidduchim*. Three years in the new yeshivah had made a tremendous difference. When potential in-laws did a background check on me, they heard only good things. Naturally, if they would've investigated a little further and asked people from my previous yeshivah, they would've rejected the suggestion right away.

I became engaged to a very fine girl. Her parents had actually asked about me at both yeshivos, but when Hashem wants something to work out, He sees to it that it does. Apparently they encountered the only two *bachurim* who knew nothing about my former problem, or if they knew, they decided not to bring it up.

I got married, we had children, and slowly my old wounds healed. I learned to accept the suffering I'd been through, and was even grateful for it, because it had changed me from an arrogant boy into a balanced young man — from a person who clings to others and tries to control them to one who understands that he mustn't smother people, not even with love or friendship in excess.

I learned the meaning of restraint, and how to achieve the right balance of closeness in a relationship.

Ten years have passed since then.

A few months ago, while I was standing in the personal-care aisle of my local supermarket, a man came up to me with a quizzical look on his face. "You look familiar," he said. "Do I know you from somewhere?" He stood there blinking and tapping his forehead, but he couldn't remember where he'd seen me before.

But I knew very well who *he* was. He the subject of my old dependency, the friend I'd wanted so much to hang on to that I'd invented a non-existent cancer in a desperate ploy to keep him attached to me. We'd both gained weight and aged somewhat, and he couldn't figure out who I was. But me? How could I forget?

For a moment, I considered telling him who I was, adding an apology, and ending the meeting graciously; but I was afraid. I'd heard that alcoholics, or people addicted to other substances, are never really "cured"; they can only call themselves "substance-free." I knew that there was still something deep within me that was liable to develop that sick dependence again.

At the same time, I felt bad. How could I just walk away and leave him wondering who I was? But I knew that thought didn't come from real consideration for his feelings, but from a latent inner wish to become friends with him again.

I had a few seconds to make up my mind, and I decided that if I opened the door to those feelings, it would be too difficult for me to close it again.

So I just smiled, shrugged, and casually said, "Maybe I look like somebody you know." Then, with a friendly nod, I moved on and reached for the shampoo.

🎬 🎬 🎬

I know that problems of dependency or co-dependency do exist in our yeshivos and seminaries.

If you think you're starting to develop feelings of over-dependence for someone, and certainly if you're already in the throes of the self-destructive behavior that comes from such dependency, then I'd advise you to do something about it now. No gradual withdrawal, no "talking things over." Just end it.

If you think someone else is becoming overly dependent upon you, then this is my advice: If you notice anything like what I've described in my story, don't try to work things out with your friend. Do yourself a favor, and do an even bigger favor for your friend, and just break off the relationship. Even if it seems cruel, take my word for it as one who has been through it: it's the most merciful thing you can do.

In my case, for example, I wasn't aware of the destruction I was wreaking with my dependency as long as I was still caught up in it; and even if I had been aware, I didn't have the strength to break it off. I was saved by my friend (and his parents), who did the job for me. In other words, the biggest act of friendship he ever did for me was to put an end to our friendship.

# Speed Trap

**M**y story, which is still fresh in my mind, has a lot to say about the way Hashem is always watching and taking care of us.

About six months ago, I was driving down a coastal highway with my family in our car.

I'll be the first to admit that I've often driven a little over the speed limit on the intercity roads. But I'm a careful driver, and I've never been in an accident. Many people agree with me that it's not the speed that counts, but how well you pay attention to the road. Is it safe to drive at the legal speed limit while listening to loud music, calling over your shoulder to tell your kids to stop bothering each other, or picking up something from the floor of the car? Isn't it better to remain constantly attentive even if you're driving fifteen miles per hour over the speed limit?

But the law is the law, and of course I don't condone driving at really high speeds.

So there I was on the road, and I stopped to fill up at one of the gas stops along the way. As I was pulling out, I saw two policemen in the distance. Instinctively, I checked my speedometer and saw that I was well within the speed limit; I had just left the gas station and hadn't yet had a chance to speed up.

But to my surprise, they were signaling to me to stop. I had no idea what they wanted, but I pulled over to the side of the road. One of the policemen then walked over to his patrol car and took something out of the front seat. I got out of my car and went over to him. He was writing out a ticket.

"What's that for?" I asked him.

"For speeding."

"Look, I don't usually like to argue," I said in a polite tone, "but this time I'm really sure I was driving well within the speed limit."

"All right, have a look at the radar reading, then," he answered.

I looked. It registered eighty-five miles per hour.

"But I was going like a snail," I protested.

"That's what they all say."

"But I really was! There must be something wrong with your radar device."

"You can say whatever you want. In court, it'll be your word against mine."

I didn't like the sound of that. He sounded like a man who *knows* he's lying.

He went on filling out his forms, and meanwhile, I noticed that his partner looked absolutely stunned.

I edged over to him and said, "Come on, let's have the truth here. You saw I was driving slowly, didn't you?"

"I'm just a volunteer," he muttered. "It's none of my business."

"Of course it's your business. How can you help him when you know he's lying like that? What kind of racket is this?"

"Sorry, I can't help you, pal," he shrugged.

I went back to the cop and asked him to give me a break, but he just tore a form out of his book and handed it to me. "For now," he told me, "your license is suspended."

"Oh, come on," I practically yelled, "this is too much!"

"You're to appear at the stationhouse tomorrow, and the chief will decide whether or not to revoke your license."

🖋️     🖋️     🖋️

I went back to my car in despair and told my wife what had happened. She declared it an outrage. "When you go up before that officer tomorrow, tell him just what happened," she said.

The next morning, I went to the police station with my defense speech all prepared, but I quickly discovered I wasn't the only one who'd been called in that day; there were about forty people in line ahead of me. One by one, they came out with sour faces as if to say, "Forget it. He's taking away everybody's license."

My turn came. I went in and launched into my speech, but he cut me off right away. "Your license is suspended for thirty days," he pronounced, "and after that you're to appear in court. Whatever you have to say for yourself, say it then."

Crestfallen like all the others, I left.

The last time I'd been punished was back in my grade-school days. And this was an awful punishment. A driver's wheels are like his feet. When you can't use your car, you feel shackled. It's terrible.

I couldn't accept it. Day and night I talked about how unfair it was, and how I couldn't deal with it. My wife said it wasn't the end of the world and reminded me that whatever happens is decreed in Heaven.

I had no other comfort, so I decided to adopt that line of

reasoning. "Obviously, for some unknown reason, Hashem doesn't want me to drive my car for a month," I said to myself. "It must be for my own good." And gradually I made peace with my situation.

For a month, I took taxis or got rides from friends. Sometimes I would let *bachurim* who had just gotten a license drive me in my car — they were practically willing to pay for the chance to drive. And they drove just the way you'd expect from a young fellow who just got his license: either they crawled along like snails, or they were crazy daredevils.

My appearance in traffic court was scheduled, and as a matter of principle, I decided to take a lawyer who specialized in traffic cases. I knew I was right, and I wasn't going to knuckle under. I told him my story, and said I suspected that somebody else had been caught on the radar and they'd pinned the blame on me.

"There's nothing you can do about it," said the lawyer. "If he'd caught you at a stop sign, you could also say, 'The cop had it in for me,' since there was no camera. But the judge will always take the policeman's word over the citizen's, unless you can find a way to damage the officer's credibility."

"If we could get that volunteer to testify," I said, "his credibility would definitely be in question."

"What volunteer?"

I told him there had been two cops standing on the road, and neither of them had a radar device in his hand. Then one of them had run to the patrol car and claimed he had proof I was speeding.

The lawyer looked thoughtful. "The very fact that he didn't write down that there was a volunteer accompanying him in the car already calls his credibility into question."

But how were we going to find out who that volunteer was?

I wanted the lawyer to contact the cop and ask him who'd been with him that day, but the lawyer said, "No, that's not the way to do it. We've got to surprise him, so he won't be able to coach the volunteer on what to say."

I asked around, using whatever connections I could find, until I managed to collect the names of five volunteers in the area. The description of one of them fit my man, and my lawyer asked him to come in for a talk.

◄         ◄         ◄

My big day in traffic court arrived. The policeman testified that I'd been going at eighty-five miles per hour, that the radar had registered it and he'd shown it to me, and that I'd even signed on the ticket. I hadn't known at the time that I wasn't supposed to sign it unless the policeman wrote that I was denying the charges.

My lawyer began asking him questions: Where were you standing, how did you see the car, what color was it, where were you when you spotted him (the cop claimed he'd been sitting in the patrol car, which was a lie), and many more questions.

Then he said he wanted to call a witness to the stand.

He went out and called in the volunteer. The cop looked shaken when he saw who it was.

My lawyer started examining the witness. "Do you know this man?"

"Yes."

"Were you with him on such-and-such a date?"

"Yes."

"And since then?"

"Since then I am no longer volunteering for the police."

"Does this decision have anything to do with the accused?"

"Yes!"

And then the witness told a story that stunned everyone in court.

✍     ✍     ✍

"A few minutes before the defendant's car came along, another car had passed by. According to the radar device it was traveling at eighty-five miles per hour. We sped after them with lights blaring and they pulled over to the side of the road just past a gas station.

"When we approached their car, there were two youths inside. The driver began pleading with us to let him off, but the policeman ignored him and began writing out a ticket. Then the other youth mentioned the name of a certain senior official on the police force and said that the man was his uncle. As soon as the policeman heard that name, he stopped writing, and said to the driver, 'Okay, I'll let you go this time, but be more careful from now on, you hear?'

"They drove away, and just then this Orthodox man came along. The policeman told me to flag him down, and he wrote out the ticket to him — the ticket that should have been given to the young guys who were speeding. He used the radar to back him up, since it registered eighty-five miles per hour, but it wasn't this man's reading.

"Afterwards I told the officer that it was unfair," the volunteer went on, "and he said to me, 'Well, he was also going too fast.'"

Then the lawyer asked him, "This story you've just told — is that the reason you stopped volunteering in the police force?"

"No, that's not the reason," he answered.

"Then what is the reason?"

"Because two weeks later, on the front page of the newspaper I saw the pictures of four young men who'd been killed in a terrible car accident, and I recognized one of them. He was the young driver in that first car we stopped, the one who should've had his license suspended. According to the newspaper, he'd been at the wheel of the car that had caused the accident."

Heavy silence fell in the courtroom. The volunteer went on speaking:

"When I realized what price had been paid for letting that young fellow off, I blamed myself for the whole thing. I felt it was a sign from Heaven, and I decided not to volunteer for the police anymore. I submitted a complaint against this policeman, but then I was given a 'friendly warning' to withdraw it. I withdrew it, but now I'm telling the truth — the whole truth."

Well, of course that testimony made quite a sensation. The judge appeared to be deliberating for a few minutes. Then he cleared his throat and announced that the case was dismissed.

The policeman who tried to frame me was brought before the Police Investigation Unit and was eventually discharged from his position.

As for me, I definitely learned something from the whole affair. It's clear to me now that what seemed to me at first to be an unbearable punishment was a sign from Heaven. Ever since then, I make sure to drive only within the speed limit. Even though I wasn't guilty of the violation they accused me of, who knows what terrible fate I might have been saved from. As for that poor young fellow who was killed, he must have thought luck was smiling on him that day, when he went off scot-free.

I hope my story will give people a fresh perspective on the Sages' dictum, "A person must say a blessing on the bad, just as he must say a blessing on the good." Sometimes, an event that looks bad to us is really the best possible thing for us.

# Unsung Hero

I was born forty years ago, and as a small child I was stricken with polio. For as long as I can remember, I've walked with a severe limp, and my legs are badly underdeveloped.

My childhood was very difficult. A disabled kid naturally doesn't fit in very well with his healthy peers, and especially a kid who walks with a terrible limp. The fact that I'd had polio and managed to walk at all was a miracle in itself. If you want to understand how hard it is, try walking on your knees, imagining that your legs keep twisting unpredictably.

I was given special crutches that included a brace to hold my legs in place. The crutches certainly made it easier to get around, but they didn't make my gait look any more graceful.

When I was twenty-five I made *aliyah* to Israel. I found a job in a factory. The work wasn't easy, but it was done sitting down. As it only required the use of my hands, I was able to do it. I thanked God that I'd found a way to earn a respectable living.

My employer was a very kind-hearted person. Every once in a while, he would ask me, "Why don't you get married?"

At first I thought he was teasing me. "Who would want to marry me?" I would retort. By then, I had made my peace with the fact that I'd always be viewed as a cripple, as an object of pity. I'd met only a few people who could accept me as an equal, and even fewer who were really interested in me.

I lived a rented, one-room apartment. No one came to visit, and no one invited me out anywhere, either — that is, except for my employer, who would invite me to his *simchahs*, for which I felt deeply indebted to him.

When I was nearly thirty, the turning point came. My boss came over to me and told me, "I've arranged for you to meet a young lady like yourself." Apparently, a good friend of his, who also owned a factory, had a female employee who was about my age, single — and was also a polio victim. It took time for me to realize that he wasn't trying to insult me, he was just trying to offer me a suitable *shidduch*. And it took even longer for him to persuade me to actually meet the girl.

Finally, I agreed.

As soon as I met Rachel, I knew right away that she was my soul mate. Interestingly, she came from the same country I had, she had the same disability, and she walked the same way.

We soon learned that our life experiences had also been much the same. Both of us had almost given up on life, but in the end had made peace with our condition. Each of us lived alone in a small apartment, and we both earned our own living doing difficult but respectable work.

Within a short time we decided to get married, despite having no furnishings for a place of our own, very little money, and very few friends.

It was our employers who came to our aid. They acted just like the parents of the bride and groom, taking all the arrangements on themselves. As businessmen, they held a meeting at a hotel one evening, where they negotiated who would pay for what. They worked out everything; they went half and half on all the expenses. And on top of it all, each of them promised several thousand dollars as a wedding gift to us. All we had to do was show up for the wedding at the appointed time and place.

However, if you want a nice wedding, you need to have people there. Between the both of us we had very few friends, and all our family was half a world away. So my boss brought his workers, his family, his neighbors and his friends, and my *kallah*'s boss did the same. Since they were both owners of large factories and had big families, it was a very nice, lively wedding. We felt like we were among our own family.

As I came up to my bride for the *bedeken*, almost everyone's eyes were misty, and afterwards, when she walked around me seven times under the *chuppah* — an arduous task for her — people were crying openly. I didn't understand why at first, but then I realized that this wasn't something you see every day — a disabled *chasan* and *kallah*, limping into their new life together. How straight and easy could their life's path be? Who could tell?

No wonder they were crying.

We received a lot of presents, and we were very happy. We were surrounded by so much warmth and support as we began our married life.

The building where we had rented an apartment was the first stone on our path. Our employers, wanting to make everything nice for us, had found us an apartment in a prestigious neighborhood. Most of our neighbors were very well-off, stuck-up, and distant from Jewish tradition. For some reason, they didn't look very kindly on the new couple that had come to live in their building, with their embarrassing limps. Maybe they thought our presence there would bring down the property values.

We didn't care what they thought. We devoted our attention to fixing up our new home, and we made it look very attractive, if I say so myself. Anyway, there was nothing for us outside our own four walls. Except for our employers, the rest of the world had never been particularly friendly to us.

A year after the wedding, our first child was born — a boy. Once again, our bosses came with their workers and families, and again they all cried when I brought my son into the covenant of Avraham Avinu.

Caring for a baby turned out to be more complicated than we'd imagined. Since both of us walk on crutches, every act that most people find simple was a challenge for us.

My wife's disability is worse than mine, and she can't pick up a baby while standing. Either she can hold the baby, or she can hold her crutches. Me, I can manage both, but it's not so easy; it requires planning. Even if you manage to lean on something, you still have to have your free crutch handy.

At first I used to kick the crutch ahead of me as I went down the stairs with the baby, until we reached the taxi waiting outside, but I saw that the neighbors didn't like it, so I found another solution: I would hold the crutch horizontally, with the baby on top of it, and lean on the banister for support. It was quite a balancing act, and a bit risky.

With time, we developed our skills and found solutions. And then we bought a car.

That was a big event for both of us. It was an old car and a cheap one, but we felt like millionaires. There I was, the crippled boy driving along in my own car, with my wife and our child in the backseat.

Getting to the car was a big production — making our way down two flights of steps with the baby and the crutches, getting the crutches into the trunk, putting the baby in his car seat, and then finally getting ourselves in and starting the car. But we were on top of the world.

After that, we were blessed with a little girl. Again there was a *simchah*, and we were already a full-fledged family. The logistics of coming and going were even harder now, but we weren't complaining. We thanked Hashem for enabling us to conquer our disability.

One night we woke up to the sound of our baby crying. She was feverish, and when we took her temperature, the thermometer registered over 104°F. We decided we'd better take her to the hospital.

We got dressed, and then we remembered that it would take us half an hour, at best, to get the kids downstairs. At any other time, I didn't mind, but not then, when my little daughter was burning up with fever.

I decided to do something I'd never done before. I went down the hall to my neighbors' door. Although it was late, I knocked. Fortunately, they were still up.

The lady opened the door. "I hate to disturb you," I began, "but my baby's temperature is over 104°F, and we have to get her to a hospital. I need someone to carry my son downstairs, while I take the baby, so it won't take half an hour."

She gave me a disdainful look and said, "People like you should think twice before you have children." And she slammed the door in my face.

Ignoring the hot tears in my eyes, I acted like a machine,

getting down the stairs as efficiently as possible. I went care-fully, because I knew I was liable to stumble and fall with my little boy. I made it downstairs in ten minutes, and then it took me another seven minutes to take the baby down to the car. I went back upstairs to help my wife down, and I hope all your environmentally-conscious readers will excuse me for leaving the motor running to keep my babies warm, considering that one of them was shaking with a high fever already.

Thankfully, there wasn't too a long wait in the emergency room at the hospital. They examined her, gave her an injec-tion to bring down the fever, gave us medicine to take with us, and sent us home.

We got home in the middle of the night, and had to go through the whole rigmarole again. Even if it had been in the middle of the day, I wouldn't have dreamed of asking the neighbors for help this time. My cheeks still burned from the insult.

🎬  🎬  🎬

A few months passed. We didn't exchange a word with our neighbor, but this wasn't much of a change, as we'd never had much to say to each other.

Late one night, at around 1:00 A.M., we and the whole neighborhood were awakened by screaming children. The liv-ing rooms of the neighboring apartments are adjacent to each other in our building, and when we looked out our living-room window, we could see our neighbors' little son standing on top of the guard rail at their window, screaming, "Imma! Imma!"

Within a few minutes, the whole neighborhood was down in the street. Everybody was shouting at the kid, "Go back inside, you'll fall!" But he paid no attention to them, and in a moment he was joined by his two siblings, who had woken up from all the noise, and now they were standing at the window, too, yelling, "Imma! Imma!"

A few neighbors went upstairs and tried to get into the apartment, but the door was locked. They knocked on the door and called to the kids to come and open it, but the kids were still at the window, facing the street, and couldn't hear the knocking. Meanwhile, the crowd down in the street stood there, looking up helplessly at the poor children.

The only way to reach them was by way of my living room, which was next to theirs. Very laboriously, I climbed onto the window ledge and made eye contact with the boy. I could see he was terrified; he realized what he'd done and he couldn't move for fear of falling.

I told him to look at me and not to look down. I started climbing onto our guard rail in order to cross over to their side.

It was relatively easy for me to swing my body over the guard rail to the outside. People like me, with crippled legs, usually have very strong arms. So, like a kid on monkey bars, I hung from the rail and, using hand-over-hand motions, I crossed over to the neighbors' side.

Suddenly, my foot knocked against the neighbors' air conditioner. I almost slipped, but I kept an iron grip with one hand on the bar and regained my balance. I kept going until I reached the boy. I held him with one hand while holding onto the guard rail with the other, and lifted him back to safety inside the living room. Then I pulled myself over the guard rail, too, and found myself in the neighbors' apartment.

From outside, I could hear the spectators cheering and whistling.

Somehow I lurched to the door, since I didn't have my crutches, and found it had been locked from the outside and there was no key.

I went back to the window and yelled down to the police-man who had just arrived that he was going to have to break down the door from the outside.

He summoned the fire department for that purpose. It took the firemen a while to break down the door. In the meantime I tried to calm the children, telling them that everything was going to be all right.

Just then a car pulled up, and the parents stepped out, all smiles after their evening out. They didn't understand what all the hullabaloo was about until they looked up and saw the light on in their living room, and firemen holding their children in their arms.

"What's going on? What happened to my kids?" the mother quavered.

"You want to know what happened to them?" asked the police sergeant. "You went out and abandoned them, that's what." And then he added the words that resonated for me, the words that, measure for measure, she was meant to hear: "Lady, I don't know who gave you a license to raise chil-dren."

Dozens of voices chimed in, "That's right, you ought to be ashamed of yourselves." "How could you be so irrespon-sible?" "If you bring children into the world, you have to take care of them."

The sergeant went upstairs with them and told them they were going to be charged with child neglect.

🎬    🎬    🎬

The mother never thanked me, and never apologized for her nastiness to me, either. That's all right, I wasn't expecting it. For me, this incident was the best proof that there's a Judge watching what we do in this world, and that the wheel is always turning.

Eventually we moved to another, much friendlier neighborhood.

These days, I have supportive people all around me, although I still prefer to be independent.

But I don't regret the years I spent in that neighborhood. They gave me a realistic perspective on life, and they helped me to appreciate the place I live in now. Sometimes you have to experience the bad before you can really appreciate the good.

# The Power of the Tongue

**M**y story spans almost ten years.

After high school I studied in one of Israel's best seminaries, where I was considered an outstanding student. I was a lively girl, with clear opinions on everything. Among my friends, I was very popular. Everyone considered me the "life of the party."

Overall, my life was good, and I was happy and content.

At the time of my story, there was a girl in my class who came from a terribly dysfunctional family; yet to look at her, you would never know. She was very bright and original, even though she did have some odd opinions. Most of us didn't agree with those opinions, but it was always interesting to hear them.

We had gotten used to her quirks, but one day during recess she outdid herself. "Today," she announced, "I'm going to tell fortunes."

If any other girl had said that, we would have just laughed and gone back to what we were doing. We laughed this time, as well, but remained where we were, because we wanted to see what she would do. She spread a colorful cloth over one of the desks and tied a gypsy's scarf around her head. Sitting down, she invited us to line up, and one by one, she would tell us what the future held in store for us.

I'm not sure why, but in a few seconds the girls were actually standing in line, waiting their turn. They must have liked the idea of a new game to play. One after the other, they sat down at the table, and she would gaze at them for a moment and then make her predictions.

Silly as the whole thing seemed at first, the girls were enjoying it. She told one girl she'd marry a rich boy, and another that she'd be the CEO of a big company. One girl was going to end up living in a foreign country, and another would get a degree in psychology. It was all taken in good humor; it was a fun to break out of our usual routine.

Sprinkled among all the silliness, though, were some piercing remarks. For example, she told the most diligent student in the class, "You're going to be a housewife" (the last thing the girl wanted to hear). And she said even worse things than that, things like, "Your marriage isn't going to last," and "When you're thirty years old, tragedy will strike." We stood around laughing at her performance, not noticing how shocked some of the girls looked when they heard these awful predictions about themselves.

Then my turn came. She looked at me and said, "The same thing that happened to Rina will happen to you."

Rina had been in our class all through elementary school and in high school, too, until she'd been forced to drop out. She had been the genius of the class.

About two years before the day I'm telling you about, she had begun acting strangely. It grew worse and worse, until she had a complete mental breakdown and had to be hospitalized. After that, she had left school completely. Every now and then we would see her in the street, talking to herself and making strange gestures. It was horrifying.

And now our "gypsy fortune-teller" was telling me that I was going to share the same fate.

My first reaction was to laugh out loud, and the girls standing around listening laughed with me. They all thought it was a good joke, apparently forgetting that it wasn't very nice to make jokes at the expense of a poor girl who had lost her mind.

"That was really good," I said, still laughing, and then the next girl in line took my place.

I slipped away to a dark corner where I could be by myself. I remember the situation very well, because that was when the big change began.

I went home feeling very strange. I was afraid I might not be walking straight, and I felt like there were voices screaming in my brain. I was so scared.

At home, I didn't speak to anybody. I went straight to bed, and that was when the long nightmare began, the nightmare that has been plaguing me ever since.

I couldn't sleep. I tossed and turned in fear, terrified that I would wake up crazy. I don't know what got into me, but apparently my classmate's statement had woken up all sorts of dark thoughts that had been lurking in the recesses of my mind, and now they were ambushing me.

I stayed home from school for a few days, claiming I didn't feel well. That was putting it mildly. I was being assaulted by terrible anxiety.

After that, I went back to school, but I wasn't the same girl I'd been. I kept telling myself I must hold on to my sanity, because if I let go, I'd lose it. I felt as if my head were about to burst from all the strange thoughts whirling around in it, and I couldn't stop them.

Soon my friends started noticing that something was troubling me, but they didn't make any connection between the fortune-telling session and the signs of distress I was showing.

One day, my best friend came up to me and said, "Listen. I can see you're going through something really hard. You've got to tell me about it."

At first, I tried to be evasive, telling her that I didn't know what she was talking about, but she wouldn't let me off the hook. Finally I couldn't pretend anymore, and I burst into tears. I told her the truth: ever since that day when our classmate had "told our fortunes," I'd been a different person. I told her I was fighting for my sanity. I wasn't able to sleep at night, and I was totally consumed with fear and anxiety.

My friend looked frightened. She was completely unprepared for something like that. She tried to calm me down by saying that the whole thing was a lot of nonsense, and I should remember that everyone looked up to me because I was so smart.

"You, of all people, the one whose opinion always counts, are afraid of going crazy?" she said.

I reminded her that the girl who'd dropped out had been the genius of the class.

"Being a genius is something else," my friend countered. "It has nothing to do with worldly wisdom or with emotional intelligence. You're a person who has her feet on the ground." It was comforting to hear that.

For all her reassurances, though, she was very disturbed by what I told her. Realizing that I might need some serious help, she urged me to see some sort of counselor. I wouldn't hear of it. Even though I knew something was wrong with me, I felt that if I went for counseling, it would be like admitting that I had a serious problem.

It took two weeks of persuasion before I agreed to go. By then, I realized that if didn't get help, I really would go crazy.

&#9209;     &#9209;     &#9209;

I told my parents what I was going through, and I began going to a psychologist. At times, she would recommend that I see a psychiatrist, who could prescribe medication, but I wouldn't agree to that. I explained to her that if I went to a psychiatrist and starting taking medication, it would just be too similar to what happened to that poor girl who used to be in our class, and I would feel like the "gypsy's predictions" had come true.

The psychologist understood this, and she helped me cope with my state of mind without resorting to drug treatment.

With her help, I managed to keep going as if everything was all right. My friends at school still thought of me as the smart, popular girl I'd always been.

It came time to start going out on *shidduchim*, and with Hashem's help I began dating a very fine boy. After we'd met several times, we got engaged.

The engagement period was very hard for me. It's a stressful time for anyone, and for me it was doubly so, because my fears of losing my mind grew worse. My worries were exacerbated by the fact that now I felt I really had something to lose. At times I was absolutely petrified, like the time my *chasan*'s family invited me for Shabbos, and somehow they got into a discussion of compulsiveness among *bachurim*. I don't know why they were talking about that, but at the time, I felt as if they were trying to hint something.

Despite everything, we got married without a hitch.

Years have passed, and today I'm the mother of three children. My husband and I have built a good Jewish home, and I work at a full-time job. And throughout all this, I'm still constantly struggling for my sanity.

I've never "gone crazy"; I've never had to be hospitalized or go on medication. To all appearances, I function normally. But my inner struggle isn't easy. Sometimes, it's more than I can bear. I have to deal with all the usual problems of life, and in addition, I have to fight this inner battle every day, every hour, against a terrible enemy that attacks my mind. I conquer my enemy each day anew and, God willing, I'll go on winning.

Words, words, words…we talk all day, yet we seldom reflect upon the fact that our speech is like a knife that can wound or even kill.

Those who think words just disappear into the airwaves and are gone, are very much mistaken. Such people can ruin lives.

Speech is like a consuming fire that burns in the soul forever, or as our Sages' said, "The tongue wields power over death and life."

Some readers will say it wasn't the "fortune-teller" who caused my troubles; she only caused a latent problem to come to the surface. This may be true, but is this the role we want to play in the world?

With a broken heart and an injured mind, I call upon all of you: Don't stir things up. Keep a guard on your speech. The tongue is like a sharp sword that can injure, maim and kill.

# The Wheel of Fortune

L ike everyone else, I read the newspaper articles about the terrible economic troubles facing the poorer sectors of our society, about families collapsing under the burden, and about people who take their own lives because the financial pressures are too much for them. When I read these things, it takes me back to an earlier period in my life.

I'm not a young man, but I vividly remember those years, and I've been thinking lately that I ought to open up and tell my story — if only for the sake of others that might be helped by it.

All this happened more than fifty years ago. I grew up in a terribly impoverished home; my parents never had a penny to spare. We lived from hand to mouth, and I constantly heard my father say, "I don't know if we're going to have anything to eat tomorrow." I'd often hear him making remarks like, "I can't go on living this way."

Those words made me very fearful. Sometimes my mother would see the fear in my eyes, and say to him, *"Nisht far der kinder!"* ("Not in front of the children!") She would then try to encourage him, telling him that soon the situation would surely get better. But my father was not at all optimistic, and his pessimism left its mark on all of us. Our house was not a very cheerful place, to put it mildly.

I had a close friend, whose family was just as poor as mine, but unlike my family, they didn't seem particularly downtrodden. My friend's father was a happy, joyful man, and the rest of the family took after him. I never heard them complaining that they lacked for anything; their home was always full of cheer. I much preferred being there to being in my own melancholy house.

My friend and I would sit and weave dreams together. We both dreamed of big, fancy houses full of all kinds of good food and treats. We would talk about setting up a business together, making lots of money, and buying ourselves all the things that our families could never afford.

When we graduated from school and went to yeshivah, we still remained close friends. However, the difference between us was obvious. He was always relaxed and carefree, while I was always anxious and worried about what was going to become of me. Yet I was still weaving my dreams, planning ways to assure myself of a good future.

A few years passed, and in time we both got married. My friend found employment as a teacher, and I worked at various temporary jobs. Yet we were both more or less on the same financial footing. Although his salary was low, it came in regularly, whereas my earnings were erratic. Sometimes I had lucrative work for awhile, but then I might find myself unemployed.

As the years passed, I felt my dreams of getting rich slipping away from me. I had two children, and I was barely managing to support my family. I became so preoccupied with making a living that I had no peace of mind.

And then, opportunity knocked. It was the big break I'd always dreamed of: Someone offered me a partnership in a food distribution business he was starting. He would provide the capital, and I would take on the bulk of the work.

We got the business up and running, and our success was meteoric. The heavens seemed to open up and flood us with riches.

In business, when you're a salaried worker, you may make a decent wage, but your income is more or less set. However, when you're a partner in the company — even though your responsibilities are greater and you may undertake some risk — there's almost no limit to what your earnings can be if your company is successful enough.

Take a forklift operator, for example. His monthly salary will be the same whether he shleps fifty thousand dollars' worth of merchandise or a hundred thousand dollars' worth. A sales agent may make a little more because of bonuses or sales incentives. But if you're the one who has the forklift operator and the sales agent on your payroll, you earn money on every item; and if you sell hundreds of thousands of items, your earnings may reach the millions.

You have expenses, of course, like paying your forklift operators and your sales agents. But if you're making even just one dollar on every item you sell, you're doing very well for yourself.

This is what happened to me after only one year in the business. I became rich, just as I'd always dreamed of. My whole lifestyle changed within that short time. I bought a beautiful house, a fancy car, and started living a life of wealth and luxury.

Meanwhile, my good friend continued teaching, enjoying

the salary increases that added a small percentage to his pay-check. He spent several years taking courses to become a certified teacher. I was amused to see how happy he was when he started making a few hundred dollars more per month due to his newly earned credentials.

As time passed, I continued to expand my enterprise. I bought up other companies along the way and became a kingpin in the food industry. But despite all the changes and the differences in our lifestyles, I kept up my relationship with my old friend.

During the 1980's, my business affairs started skidding, through no fault of my own. A big food-chain collapsed; when they declared bankruptcy, their debt to me was in the hundreds of thousands.

Since I could no longer collect on it, and my bank knew it, I began to have cash flow problems of my own. I couldn't pay the importers and local suppliers, and very soon my bank stopped honoring my checks.

If I'd been on the production end of the food business, I might have had a chance to save myself, because I could have kept on making my products and selling them. But since all my profits depended on buying and selling, I was in trouble. My business assets consisted mainly of warehouses and office buildings.

With no available cash, everything grinds to a halt. You can't buy if no one will sell to you on credit. You can't sell, because your clients don't pay; and even if they do, the bank freezes the funds anyway. Besides, if you can't buy, you have no merchandise to sell. And if you can't pay your salesmen, they won't work for you.

My whole business actually revolved around one thing —

my good name. And when you get into trouble with your bank, your good name disappears overnight. Very soon, word spread in the industry that I couldn't pay my debts and that my employees were quitting left and right.

The downfall hit me very hard. It wasn't only my pockets that were hurting. At times like those, you find out just how fickle people can be. The very same people who worked in your favor, putting you ahead of all your competitors, now suddenly work against you, leaving you in the lurch. The banks that were so eager to have your business that they would offer you special terms and low-interest rates, turn out to be the first to look at you with distrust when the chips are down, and it's their behavior that actually triggers your downfall. It was at that point that I truly understood what people mean when they talk about "the wheel of fortune."

But the hardest part of all, the thing that really tore me to pieces, was the sudden change in my standard of living.

It is written that if a rich man loses his wealth and requires the charity of others, it isn't enough to give him a few coins so that he won't starve; the community must sustain him at the level to which he was accustomed. Specifically it says that they must provide him with a horse to ride on and a servant to run before him. I could never understand that concept and, in fact, I recoiled from it. Why on earth should the community pay for a servant to run before this formerly wealthy man while he rides a horse?

But when I found myself in that man's shoes, I understood. A rich man gets used to his standard of living, and he needs it just as a poor man needs his bread and water. You grow accustomed to spending money left and right, and never having to worry about how much things cost. If you get used to having a beautiful, new car, it's practically impossible to go back to driving a beat-up, old jalopy.

But this is what I was forced to do. I had to sell all the cars I owned and buy an old rattletrap instead. It was so heartbreaking for me; I could hardly see a reason to get out of bed in the morning.

That was when I began to see how uncomplicated and carefree my old friend's life was. He'd never had a car or a high standard of living, so he didn't have to worry about experiencing a downfall. He tried to offer me encouragement. He was right when he said that even at that point I was still living on a higher standard than him, but his words went in one ear and out the other. I couldn't take any joy in what I still had left, I was too busy eating my heart out over what I'd lost.

Those were tough days. I didn't know if I'd ever get out of the deep depression I was in. I felt I'd lost everything, overlooking all the treasures I still had — my wife, my children, my friends, my house. All I thought about was my financial situation, and I couldn't bear it. I prayed to God that He should help me, because I couldn't take it anymore.

I'm ashamed to recall the state I sank into during that period. I was like a zombie. My wife and children were walking on eggshells around the house, worried and afraid of disturbing me. They didn't know what to do. My wife would say, "Please, go to shul, at least for the children's sake. You can't just lie there like that all the time."

"I can't," I'd say. "I don't have the strength. I have nothing left to live for."

"Look at the children," she pointed out, trying to cheer me up. "Look at how well they're doing, how talented they are. They don't need a lot of money. All they want is a healthy, happy father."

Maybe I was too selfish, or more likely it was just weakness, but I didn't even hear what she was saying.

☐　　☐　　☐

My depression couldn't be kept a secret in our community for long. My friends soon discovered what had happened and that I was suffering from a mental crisis. They must have gotten together to figure out how they could help me. They started a fundraising drive that I didn't know about, or maybe I should say that I didn't want to know about.

My best friend got a committee of friends together and they met with me to clarify the extent of my debts; then they negotiated for me with my bankers and creditors to work out a feasible payment schedule. The committee required of me that I refrain from writing any checks or making any expenditure without their authorization. It made me feel like a dependent child, with my friends as the parent figures. But I must say they handled the matter with respect and sensitivity. It was the only way they could rescue me from my plight.

Within a year, they managed to pay off my debts, which had been my biggest obstacle to rising up out of the slump I was in. After that, I started working as a sales agent for one of the companies I'd worked with in the past. It wasn't easy. At first, I didn't put much energy into it; I felt like I was only doing it because I had no choice in the matter. But I gradually got used to the idea, and I began to make some money.

Meanwhile, court proceedings were underway against the company that had caused me to go bankrupt. True, they had also gone bankrupt, but they had valuable assets such as buildings and other property, and my lawyer, along with attorneys representing other creditors, was demanding a share of those assets for me.

The machinery of justice chugs along slowly. It took five

years, but eventually an arrangement was made with the creditors, and each of us received a nice sum of money. It was less than a third of what they actually owed me, but it was enough to get me set up in business again.

I returned to food distribution, and I made a big comeback. It wasn't like before, but I was taking a safer approach this time around — relatively speaking, that is, because nothing in business is risk-free, and certainly not in the food business.

Today, I'm financially well-off once again. I've married off most of my children, helping them get a nice start in life, and I've also helped the people who helped me when I was going through tough times. I owe a lot to them.

✍ ✍ ✍

As a businessman who has suffered a crash and then recovered, I feel qualified to address those of you who are in financial straits, or who might be faced with such a situation in the near future. When my life was at its low point, if someone would have told me that the day would come when I'd recover my losses and marry off my children respectably, that I'd have *nachas* from them and enjoy beautiful grandchildren, I wouldn't even have answered him. My mind was too impervious at the time even to entertain such notions. But now, looking back on that time, I'm surprised at how short-sighted I was.

I'm reminded of the story that I read in one of your books about a woman who was in a state of deep despair, until she met another woman who told her that life's path is full of twists and turns. When there's no solution in sight, its because the solution is hidden just around the next bend. I believe that's very true, but I'll say even more than that: Often, the twists and turns themselves are created by our own imagination. In my case, for example, I was never really in such a terrible situation. I wasn't threatened by some awful fate; I just had to go back to living the way I did before I became rich. But my mind tricked me into thinking that it was the end of the world. It's these twists and turns that lead us to understand that life is a gift.

Now, as a father and grandfather who's happy with his portion, I know enough to thank Hashem and appreciate all His gifts to me — my wife, my children, and my old friend — together with the gift of life.

# *Hit and Run*

I t is *motza'ei Shabbos* as I sit down to write this letter.
We've just finished a "three-day Yom Tov," with the two
days of Rosh Hashanah falling out on Thursday and Fri-
day. These three days have given me plenty of time to think.
The thoughts that occurred to me during these days of reflec-
tion are what prompted me to sit down now and write.

During the Rosh Hashanah prayers I was full of praise and
thanks to Hashem for the great kindness He showed me this
past year, and all of a sudden, I felt a strong urge to put my
story in writing. I have two reasons for this: first, to express
my gratitude to Hashem, and second, to offer encouragement
to others who are in the position I was in and think their fate
is sealed. They should keep in mind our Sages' saying that
even if a sharp sword is placed at a person's neck, he should
not despair of Hashem's mercy.

I'm going back nearly a year in time now, back to the
eleventh of Tishrei 5764, the day after Yom Kippur, 2003.

I was at home in Jerusalem, in the midst of my preparations for Sukkos, when suddenly a police van pulled up

outside my house. Two policemen jumped out, came up to my door and told me, "You're under arrest."

"What?" I said, stunned. "For what?"

"You'll hear about that at the stationhouse," they said.

There was nothing I could do. Before the eyes of my wife, my children, and all my neighbors, I was taken away in handcuffs to the police station.

I sat there for a few hours without being told what I'd been arrested for. Then they brought me into an interrogation room, and the police detective started asking me where I was on a certain date (about a month previous). I tried to think back to that day, but I couldn't remember where I was, so I told him I didn't know. He took that to mean I was trying to avoid answering, and he started yelling that I'd better tell him the truth. I told him I didn't know what he wanted from me.

From his questions, I gathered that the charges against me had something to do with my car. He asked me about the model, the color and the license plate number, and if I was driving in a certain location on a certain date. Since I do occasionally drive through the street he was talking about, I couldn't say for sure that I hadn't been there. So I just said I had no idea if I'd been there on the date they were talking about.

After he tried to get me all confused and to put words in my mouth that I hadn't said, I stopped him and asked him to tell me just what I was being charged with. Another policeman came into the room at that point, and they both started screaming at me, "Are you trying to play games with us? What kind of heartless animal are you? You injured someone seriously, and now you're trying to play innocent?"

As soon as I heard that, I felt relieved. I said to them,

"Maybe I was speeding a little, or maybe I went through a stop sign, but if you're saying I was in an accident — no. You've got the wrong man."

"Just a moment," they said. "You're confessing that you went through a stop sign and that you were speeding?"

"I'm not confessing anything," I said. "All I meant was that I thought you had me here for some kind of traffic violation."

"But you just said you were speeding. Was that a lie?"

"I've had enough of this," I said to them. "I see that you're not interested in the truth. You arrest an innocent man and try to frame him for a serious crime. I'm not saying another word to you from here on; I have a right to remain silent."

They took a scornful view of my legal rights. "Oh, you have a right to remain silent, do you? Just who do you think you are — the prime minister's son?" (Gilad Sharon, the son of the Israeli prime minister, was in the headlines at the time for keeping silent in an investigation against his father.)

"All right, remain silent as long as you like," they said. "We'll throw you into solitary until you beg us to let you talk."

I said nothing.

"Will you sign the testimony?"

I said nothing.

That made them mad. They started screaming their heads off, and then one of them pushed me up against the wall.

I kept quiet. I didn't say, "Hey, keep your hands off." Once I'd made up my mind to remain silent, I remained silent.

With a lot of pushing, shoving and insults, they brought me through the corridors to a little room, and locked the door behind me. There were several other men in the room.

I was feeling pretty antagonistic by then, and as the police left, I felt like calling after them, "Hey, you promised me solitary!" But since I'd promised to keep silent, that's what I did.

☙        ☙        ☙

I looked around for a bed. There were a few berths with mattresses, and my roommates were sitting around on them.

I sat down, too, and somebody asked me, "What are you here for?" I wanted to pour out my heart and say I was being falsely accused of a crime, but instead, I did the smarter thing and said, "Don't interfere with my life, so I won't have to interfere with yours."

That was a risky thing to say, since he looked like the sort of guy I really wouldn't want interfering with my life, and if he decided to call my bluff, I probably wouldn't have much of a life left. But the risk paid off. He looked at me for a long time, and didn't say anything more. I guess he decided I was a tough guy, and he'd better look for easier prey.

In the evening they brought me before a judge for extension of custody. When my turn came, the prosecutor said, "Your honor, the defendant is accused of running over a five-year-old girl in a hit-and-run accident one month ago." He gave details about the car, the date and time, and the location.

The judge asked me what I had to say for myself. "Your honor, I'm innocent," I said. "This is the first time that I've even heard what I'm being accused of."

The prosecutor said, "The accused admits that he was at the scene of the crime, that he was speeding, and that he failed to stop at a stop sign."

"That's a lie!" I shouted. "I never said that!"

"Your honor, it was all taken down in the prisoner's statement."

"It's all lies. Show me my signature on that statement."

"Your honor, the prisoner refused to sign the statement. As soon as he was told what he was being charged with, he claimed the right to remain silent."

"Your honor," I said, "I claimed the right to remain silent because they were saying I confessed to the crime."

The judge ruled to extend my custody for seven days, and said that I would see a lawyer within twenty-four hours.

"Next case," he said.

◄       ◄       ◄

They took me back to my holding cell, and all at once, I understood how the judicial system works. If the judge had asked me another question or two, he would have been able to see my side. But he didn't ask; he just made a decision by rote to extend my custody for seven days.

The next day, I was summoned again for interrogation. I wanted to explain my position to them, but after what had happened the day before, I felt I couldn't trust them. They shot hundreds of questions at me, threatening me with a harsh prison sentence, but I remained silent. I wouldn't even tell them my name or ask them to open the window because it was stifling in there.

Two hours later, I met with a lawyer. My wife had gone to our neighborhood *rav*, and he had hired this lawyer for me.

"I'm absolutely innocent," I told the lawyer. "You've got to get me out of here."

"That's a tall order," he said to me. "They claim it was a hit-and-run accident, and a little girl was badly hurt. They have statements from witnesses who saw the car and the license plate number. They're very sure of their case against you."

"Look, Mr. Lawyer," I said, "if you don't believe me, you'd

better leave right now and send me another lawyer instead. I didn't run over any little girl. I didn't even run over a cat. There's some terrible mistake here."

"There's a big uproar over this case," the lawyer said. "The story's in the papers. They say you're claiming the right to remain silent. What are you remaining silent for, if you didn't do anything wrong?"

"If you'll hear me out, I'll explain," I said. And I told him what they'd done during the interrogation, what I'd said and how they'd tried to put words in my mouth and turn it into a confession that I was supposed to sign, and how, after I wouldn't sign it, the judge had extended custody for a week.

At this point, he started getting mad, too. "I'll be filing a request within the next twelve hours to have you released," he said.

🎬     🎬     🎬

I was brought before the judge again. My lawyer presented my side of the story and confronted the policemen head on. He demanded access to all the evidence they had against me, and requested that the judge release me on bail.

The judge was impressed by the way my lawyer presented my side of the story; but still, he said, there were testimonies that connected me with the accident, and therefore, I would be detained another twenty-four hours, during which time the lawyer could prepare a refutation of the charges.

I was transferred to a regular prison, where I made the acquaintance of some fine fellows who I wouldn't recommend touching with a fifty-foot pole.

I began to lose hope; my whole world went dark. Somebody surely must have seen a car just like mine. They weren't going to believe me. I was afraid I was going to have to serve a prison sentence even though I wasn't guilty. It must have been decreed by Heaven, I thought.

The other inmates recognized me. "We saw you in the paper today," they said. "So you hit a little girl and ran, eh?"

When they said that, I thought of my wife, my children, and my parents, and the awful shame they must be suffering.

A hearing on my case was held the next day. My lawyer began by asking the prosecutor, "You say that on the date in question the accused was seen at the scene of the accident?"

"Yes," the prosecutor replied. "We have eye witnesses to that effect, as well as private investigations that we carried out."

"Well, I have exhibits and testimonies to prove that the accused, and his car, were in another place at that time, over a hundred miles away from the scene of the crime."

That came as a surprise even to me. Where had I been a month ago that was so far away?

"You say that the accident occurred at approximately 7:00 P.M. that evening?"

"Yes, it did."

"Well, the accused was with his family that day, visiting the gravesites of the *tzaddikim* in the north of the country, They did not return to Jerusalem until after 11:00 P.M., and the car in question is the vehicle that took them there and back."

I was in shock. That was right! Or at least, we did take a trip up north some time around that day.

"Do you have evidence to prove that statement?"

"I certainly do," said my lawyer. "So far, I've collected ten pieces of evidence, and I expect to have more in the next few days. For now, I will present what I have."

First, he exhibited receipts, with the date indicated, from various places we'd visited that day. (I have a habit of keeping receipts.) But this wasn't a strong enough proof. After all, we could have gotten the receipts from friends in the area.

Next, he exhibited photographs we took that day, showing the date in the lower corner of each one. But again, the proof wasn't conclusive. Maybe someone had changed the date setting on the camera and taken the pictures some time after the accident?

Then he called in a witness. The attendant of a rabbi that we'd gone to see on the way, stated that he remembered me, and that I was there on the day in question. But the judge wasn't willing to put too much faith in that. In any case, that had been early in the day.

And then, the lawyer took out a receipt for a purchase made on my credit card at 6:30 in the evening. It was from a gas station located in the Galilee region, and it clearly showed both my credit card number and my license plate number. Now we had definite proof that my car was up north at the time of the accident.

That stumped the prosecutor. He asked to see the receipt, and looked it over carefully. He asked the judge to allow him a few days to check into the matter. He claimed it was possible that someone else had used my credit card that day.

The judge looked interested, but my lawyer was quick to squash that idea. "The car's number appears on the receipt, too," he said. "The number of the car that supposedly hit the child half an hour later, over a hundred miles away."

The prosecutor had an answer to that, too: "The gas station attendant asks for a number. The driver can give him any number he wants."

That got me hopping mad. "Your honor," I said, "you've got clear proof here of my innocence. Why would somebody else, in a different car, want to give my license plate number to the gas station attendant?"

The judge told me to sit down and be quiet.

⚑        ⚑        ⚑

Next, to my surprise, my lawyer called another witness to the stand... the gas station attendant. The lawyer, it seems, had gone personally to the gas station and questioned all the attendants until he found one who remembered me.

The attendant took the stand and my lawyer asked him to tell the court what connection he had to me, the defendant.

He said that he remembered that I'd been at the gas station on the day in question. He said he couldn't testify to the exact time, but that when he'd been shown a picture of the car and a picture of me, he recognized us.

The judge asked him, "Out of thousands of customers who come into your gas station, how can you claim to recognize this man?"

"Because he gave me a big tip," the attendant replied. "Only about one in a hundred customers even gives a tip at all."

"But why should this one man stand out in your memory?"

"Because he was driving such an old car. And I could see from all the kids inside that he had a large family," the attendant answered. "I remember thinking to myself that he probably needs the money more than I do." Everyone laughed.

But the judge wasn't satisfied. "Yet isn't it possible that you might be confusing him with someone else?" he asked. "Or perhaps that it happened on a different day and not necessarily on the day of the accident."

"It's true that I might not have remembered him just

because of the big tip," the witness admitted, "but there was something else — something I couldn't forget."

"What was that?" my lawyer asked.

"He asked me, 'Are you Jewish?'

"I told him yes. And then he said, 'You know, it's Elul now, the month when Jews do *teshuvah*. I'm not trying to turn you into a *ba'al teshuvah*, I just thought that since you're Jewish, you'd like to know what the Jews do this month."

Silence fell in the courtroom. The judge was undecided. It was a nice story, but there were still holes in it. After a moment of silence, during which the prosecutor tried to speak but was hushed by the judge.

After a few tense moments the judge finally said, "Since the accused doesn't look like a dangerous person, and since evidence has been presented, even if that evidence is not conclusive, indicating that he was not at the scene of the crime, I rule that the accused be released on bail. The defense has one month in which to present more conclusive evidence to clear him of the charges."

I was released on bail, and within ten days my lawyer managed to establish that the evidence the police had against me was unreliable. Their "eye witnesses" had seen the car that hit the child, and were able to make out only part of the license plate number. The police had looked for a car that matched the description, and when they found my car they tried to build a case against me. In the end, the charges were dropped for lack of evidence.

My release was written up in a short item in the newspaper, but still… still the suspicion hovered over me. They let me go because they had no conclusive proof, but my innocence hadn't been clearly established, either.

Only in Elul 5764, a year after the accident, did the truth come to light. That was when the real culprit was caught for another crime, and under interrogation he confessed that he was the hit-and-run driver who had injured the girl a year previously.

He had an old Subaru the same color as mine, and the last numbers on his license plate were also identical to mine. But all the rest of the details were totally different.

On Rosh Hashanah, I was able to stand cleansed and exonerated in the eyes of both God and man. I could only thank Hashem, Who releases the imprisoned, for the great kindness He performed for me and my family.

# Angels at a Wedding

L ast week, I took part in a very special wedding, and I feel the need to share the story behind it with you and with your readers.

The story began some twenty-five years ago. Perhaps it really began long before that.

I'm a native of Haifa, and I belong to a congregation called Ahavas Torah. Our shul is at the junction of Arlozarov and Yosef Streets. It's a *kehillah* of German Jews, otherwise known as *yekkes*.

One of the friends I grew up with was Aryeh Strauss. His family also belonged to our shul. After elementary school, we went our separate ways, moving on to different yeshivos, but we still ran into each other in shul from time to time when we were both home for a Shabbos or *bein hazmanim* vacation.

Aryeh was a tall, handsome boy, very strong physically and with an outstanding personality to boot.

He was named after an uncle who had fought in the Israeli War of Independence. His uncle died in that war, from a bullet wound to the head.

Aryeh got married at a rather young age to a local girl, whose family also *davened* in our shul — the Dreyfus family.

Strauss and Dreyfus are both very prominent *yekke* names. So it was a match made in Heaven. They were so well suited — both of them outstanding young people from excellent families, and both had received the best upbringing and education.

About a year later, Aryeh's wife gave birth to a son, whom they cared for lovingly. Aryeh and his wife blossomed both as a couple and as parents.

And then came 1982, and war broke out in Lebanon. Aryeh Strauss was called up to serve in an armored tank unit. In the infamous battle at Sultan Yakub, a shell hit Aryeh in the head, killing him instantly, just as his uncle — after whom he'd been named — had been killed more than three decades earlier.

His young wife was left a widow, with a year-and-a-half-old son who'd barely had a chance to know his father.

I'll never forget how terribly he was mourned. Aryeh was one of those nearly perfect human beings. Like many others of his caliber, it seems that Hashem decided he was too perfect to stay on in this imperfect world of ours, and he was taken to a better place.

About a year later, Aryeh's parents had a talk with their daughter-in-law. "You're such a young woman," they told her. "You're still at the beginning of your life. You need a husband, and your son needs a father. It's time for you to remarry."

They weren't satisfied with mere words; they began looking for a *shidduch* for her, exactly as if she were their own daughter. Eventually, they found a good match, a young doctor around Aryeh's age, by the name of Sachs.

The Strausses came to the wedding, of course, and they regarded Dr. Sachs as a son, just as they regarded the bride as their daughter.

The new couple went on to have more children, whose good fortune it was to have three sets of grandparents: Dreyfus, Sachs and Strauss.

From the beginning, Dr. Sachs set out to make sure the little boy would not forget his father. He placed a big picture of Aryeh next to the child's bed, and every year on the *yahrtzeit* he went with him to the cemetery to say *Kaddish*.

He would tell the boy stories about his father that illustrated what a special person he was, how diligently he studied the Torah and how careful he was in performing the mitzvos. He told him what a brave soldier his father had been and how he'd died a martyr's death defending the Jewish People.

Aryeh's son grew up proud of his deceased father and was surrounded by warmth and love from his mother and stepfather. He matured into a fine young man, went to learn in yeshivah, and then got married.

This was the wedding I spoke of at the beginning of this letter. I hardly have words to describe the joy and poignancy of that wedding. So many tears were shed there!

As the young man walked to the *chuppah*, a recording of his father singing, twenty years earlier to another *chasan* and *kallah*, played in the background. I don't know where they got the recording from.

Right behind the couple were the Dreyfus and Sachs families, as well as Savta Strauss (unfortunately Aryeh's father had already passed on). Everyone present knew what amazing minds and hearts had been at work here, and how they had succeeded, through their wise approach, in preserving the father's memory in his son's consciousness.

Rabbi Yitzchak Zilberstein of Bnei Brak was the *mesader kiddushin*. After the blessings had been recited, he gave a short speech:

"*Raboisai*, don't you see? There are angels here, around this *chuppah*. Can you not sense it?

"The holy martyr, Reb Aryeh Strauss is here, may Hashem avenge his blood, and he is purer than any of us; for there is purity even greater than that which is attained by immersing in a *mikveh*, and that is purification by fire. Reb Aryeh passed through a *mikveh* of fire, the purest thing imaginable, and he is here with us, accompanying his son to the *chuppah*."

Rabbi Zilberstein paused for a moment, and then continued. "And there is another angel here — Dr. Sachs, who raised this boy in place of his father. And not only did he take care not to overshadow the child's memory of his father, he went further than that and actively cultivated the deceased father's legacy, while offering his own as well. Don't you see? There are real angels present here.

"And the mother," Rabbi Zilberstein added, "the widow who gathered up her strength, re-established her family, and raised the son of her first marriage together with the rest of her children — she is another angel."

After another brief pause, Rabbi Zilberstein mentioned one more angel, bringing tears to everyone's eyes: Mrs. Strauss, Reb Aryeh's mother, who stood firm and strong, never wavering. "This is a true angel," said the *rav*. "A woman of wisdom and sterling character, who put aside her personal feelings and acted with true nobility. She said to her daughter-in-law, 'You must remarry,' and helped her to find a new marriage partner, and in the process she gained more grandchildren who call her 'Savta.'"

Everyone there was moved to tears, including the *chasan* and *kallah* — and including yours truly, the writer of these words.

I would like you to tell this story in your next book. Try to convey some inkling of the emotion we felt at that wedding, so that it can serve as an example of how noble-spirited people act in accordance with their best *middos*. Let the story serve to elevate the soul of my friend, the pure martyr, Reb Aryeh Strauss, may Hashem avenge his blood, and may he merit eternal life.

# It's Never Too Late

About two years ago, I read a story of yours in *People Speak* entitled "Pay Them Back." In the story, two girls who had caused pain to their classmate ended up being punished by Hashem because they hadn't asked her forgiveness.

The story really struck a chord, because I myself have been nursing an old wound for fifty-five years. When I read "Pay Them Back," my own painful story came back to me vividly.

As a child, I was a quiet girl, unassuming and very naïve.

One day when I was about eight years old, my older sister showed me some pictures she'd been collecting. They were pictures of popular singers, and my sister said it was a very valuable collection.

Those were more innocent days, you see, and there was less awareness of the need to put up barriers against the surrounding culture. People simply didn't give it that much thought.

Personally, I wasn't very interested in music, and certainly not in pictures of pop singers, but since my sister had said it was a valuable collection, I was excited about it.

She asked me to keep the pictures in my schoolbag. I didn't understand why, but I didn't mind keeping them for her.

At school the next day, I told five of my classmates I had something special to show them, and excitedly, I took out the pictures, explaining that they were very valuable. I was really just parroting everything my sister had said, spicing it up with my own enthusiasm.

I can still remember what a significant event this was for me. I'd always been introverted, because I never felt I had anything to contribute to a group, but now I had something special to offer. It didn't matter what it was; the important thing was that suddenly, I was the center of attention, with other girls all around me, interested in hearing what I had to say.

One of the girls warned me that if the teacher found out I had pictures like that in my possession, I would be expelled. It was a religious school, you see, and she told me that I wasn't allowed to bring such pictures to school. I was shocked; never in my life had I broken a school rule. And even though I didn't really see what was wrong with the pictures, her comment worried me — I didn't want to get in trouble.

However, my concern was eclipsed by the attention I was receiving from the other girls. For me, this was sort of a rite of passage, an initiation to social acceptance, and if it had turned out well, I might have been a different person today — more sociable and less of an introvert.

But my initiation ended in disaster.

144

After recess, as soon as we were settled in the classroom, the teacher announced that she would be conducting a search of all our schoolbags.

An awful feeling came over me. I knew I had something to hide, but there was no way I could hide it.

The teacher didn't waste any time. She came straight over to me, picked up my bag and turned it over, shaking out all the contents.

One after the other, the glossy, black-and-white pictures came sliding out.

She picked up each picture separately, asking me every time, "What is this?" and "What is this?"

The other girls giggled and shook their heads at me. I'd always been in my quiet little corner, and now, in one instant, I'd turned into a laughingstock.

The teacher tore the pictures to bits, threw them on the floor, and told me to clean up the mess. There I was, shamed and humiliated, picking up the pieces of my treasure, crying out of wounded pride. When I was finished, she sent me home.

Any chances I had of ever changing were demolished that day. After that incident, I lost the courage to try to overcome my shyness.

I drew three conclusions from that incident:

- When you stand out and have people listening to you, that's bad.
- Don't trust anyone. (Obviously, someone had tattled on me.)
- Avoid taking any initiative, because you never know if your actions will cause you unanticipated humiliation.

In adolescence, I continued playing my childhood role, keeping to the sidelines in any social setting. I grew up and got married to an introvert like myself, and we lived a quiet, peaceful life together.

⬛    ⬛    ⬛

Throughout all those years, hardly a day passed when I didn't think about that painful incident with my teacher. I knew I had broken a rule by bringing those pictures to school, but with every passing day it became clearer and clearer to me that if the teacher had called me aside and asked a few probing questions, she would have discovered that the whole thing had been done in innocence. She could have explained to me why the pictures were inappropriate and taken them away from me quietly, and I would even have agreed to it.

I was just an innocent little girl and she had wronged me, not even taking the trouble to find out if I was really at fault.

On top of that, she had put me to shame. Even if I'd done something improper, did she have to humiliate me like that?

On only a few occasions did my husband ever see me cry, and every one of those occasions was when I talked about that experience. And he wasn't the only one who heard about it. There were four or five times when I spoke about it to friends or in a support group. Each time I recalled the incident, it brought on a flood of tears.

When the first volume of *People Speak* came out, I read the story I mentioned earlier. I could really empathize with the injured party's feelings. I understood why that girl couldn't forgive the ones who'd hurt her. I knew that I hadn't forgiven my grade-school teacher, either.

But it didn't occur to me to try to track her down, because I thought she must have departed from this world years ago. I remembered her as a mature woman, when she taught my class, and this was fifty-five years later.

⬛    ⬛    ⬛

And then, just a few months ago, I read an article you wrote. You explained that forgiving helps the injured party to overcome his pain — because when a person asks forgiveness from someone, he acknowledges responsibility for hurting that person, which alleviates the latter's pain.

That was a novel way of looking at it, I thought, because usually people talk about it the other way around — stressing the need for the one who inflicted the injury to be forgiven.

But I liked the idea, and it got me thinking once again about my teacher, and about the fact that she'd never apologized for what she'd done.

As I said, I had assumed she was no longer among the living. After all, I wasn't young anymore myself, and she was much older. But the memory was still haunting me, and one day when I had a free moment, I opened the local telephone book to look up her number. I knew which street she had lived on, and when I found the right page in the directory, there was her name, still listed at the same address.

Scared and hesitant, I called the number. I thought one of her grown children, who'd inherited the apartment from her, might answer, and it would be awkward asking for her.

After a few rings, an elderly woman answered. "Mrs. Rabinowitz?" I asked.

"This is she," came the answer.

I then asked her if she had ever taught in the elementary school I'd attended, and she said that she had taught there for her entire teaching career, until she retired.

It turned out that she wasn't as old as I'd thought. She was now seventy-eight. When she'd taught my class, she'd been only twenty-three years old. To my childish eyes she'd appeared to be middle-aged, but in fact, she was only fifteen years my senior.

I told her my name and asked if she remembered me. She

said yes, and she even named one or two other girls who'd been in the class with me, and said that I'd been a good, quiet pupil.

A bit haltingly, I told her why I was calling — that she'd hurt me one day when I was her pupil, and that all these years the pain of that incident had been eating away at my heart. I'd decided, I said, that I should let her know about it, and tell her I'd like her to ask me for *mechilah*.

She asked me to tell her what she'd done to hurt me, and I told her the old story. She couldn't recall the incident, but she said if that is what had happened, then she was certainly very sorry.

She asked me very nicely to forgive the injury, and said that it wouldn't have happened that way if it had ever occurred to her that I'd only made an innocent mistake. She also admitted that even if I'd done it on purpose, she should not have put me to shame like that.

I didn't lash out at her; and when we ended the conversation she apologized once again, and I said I forgave her.

Ever since that moment, I've felt so much better, as if a heavy weight has been removed from my heart. Now, when I recall that incident, it no longer hurts so much. That searing sense of humiliation is gone. Being asked for forgiveness and granting it, has put some distance between me and the original experience.

I'm writing this in order to thank you for the idea that brought me so much relief from my pain, and also in order to encourage people to speak up and ask forgiveness from anyone they've hurt.

And more than that: People who've been hurt should speak up, too. They should open up the way for others to ask forgiveness from them. It might seem a bit haughty to tell others that they should ask you for forgiveness, but if it's done in the right way, it brings healing.

It's a human need to want to hear an apology when we've been hurt, and we should permit ourselves to feel that need and seek to be understood.

# Cast Your Bread

Everyone needs to earn a living somehow, and I earn mine by driving a tow truck.

On the face of it, it seems a pretty straight-forward, boring kind of job: Hook up a car, and drag it from Point A to Point B. But the reality is more complex than that. For one thing, there isn't necessarily any easy access to Point A, and Point B isn't always the garage you were told you were taking the car to.

I've had calls from people who just wanted to collect insurance money and wanted me to spirit their vehicles away in the dark of night so they could report them as stolen. I make it clear to those people that I'm an honest person and would never do anything illegal.

It's true that much of the time the calls I receive are to tow cars that have broken down or just won't start for whatever reason. But sometimes, the calls are much more interesting. And when I'm called to tow away vehicles that have been involved in accidents, the scene that greets me there can be downright frightening.

The story I'm about to tell you is certainly interesting, and definitely very frightening.

✐      ✐      ✐

One night I receive a call at about 2:00 A.M. Since I offer 24-hour-a-day service, I answer the call as usual. The caller's car has broken down on a road in the West Bank.

Some tow-truck drivers won't work over the Green Line. Because of the Intifada, they consider it too dangerous. But that doesn't scare me off, so I tell them that I'll come within the hour.

When I get there, I see a little Peugeot sedan, and next to it — I'm not exaggerating — an Arab family of about fifteen people. Dad, Mom and kids, who appear to range in age from newborn to about eighteen.

"What happened?" I ask them.

"We don't know, our car just died on us," they answer. "We've been stuck here since ten o'clock."

I ask them where they live, and they name an Arab village which is known to be a terrorist hot-bed. That's where they want me to take their car.

I don't ask questions. I load up their car and start moving.

But then I stop and say, "And how are you people going to get home?"

They look at me, all bewildered. "We don't really know," they say. "We've been trying to hitch a ride, but nobody's stopping for us."

I think for a moment, and then I think twice. "All right," I say. "Get into the tow truck."

There are only two seats in the cabin of a tow truck, but in a pinch you can squeeze in up to five people.

The rest of the kids, I pack into *their* car, which I'm towing.

151

They don't bat an eye. After all, they all had been in that car until a few hours ago. If they could drive that way, they could certainly be towed that way.

◀   ◀   ◀

I head for their village, an hour's drive from the spot. They give me directions, and I drop them off in front of their house.

They thank me sincerely, and then, suddenly, somebody calls out, "Where's Jalal?"

It looks as if somebody's missing.

They're searching for Jalal. Maybe he's somewhere in the car, asleep, or maybe he's in the driver's cabin. But Jalal is nowhere to be found. That means we must have left him behind way back there on the Tisi Nabi road, in the middle of Samaria.

Jalal, they tell me, is a three-year-old boy. That means there's a good chance of him running out into the road as if it were a playground.

"Send someone with me," I tell them, "and I'll bring him."

They look at me in disbelief. I'm sure they never dreamed I'd offer to do that.

They send their eldest son, Ataf. We drive off together, an hour's trip.

Ataf is silent all the way. He looks hostile. So I keep quiet and continue driving. I'm not one to wake up sleeping dogs, especially if they look angry, too.

We reach the spot at last. Jalal is right there where we left him, with his head leaning on a rock, crying.

Ataf says, "Jalal, we're here. We came to take you home."

Jalal starts hitting him with his little fists. He's angry, and he wants to know why the whole family ran away with the *Yahud*. (That's the Arabic word for "Jew.")

Ataf doesn't get upset. He picks up Jalal, puts him on the seat in the truck, and we drive off again. An hour later, we reach the village. Without a word, Ataf and his brother get out of the truck. No "thank you"s, no goodbyes.

Dad, in his pajamas, throws me kisses from the doorway of his house.

I'm exhausted as I head for home. It's now five in the morning, and I've spent my whole night on little Jalal and his big brother who didn't even say thank you. Is that the kind of treatment I deserve?

I just shrug it off, go home, and forget the whole episode.

☙     ☙     ☙

Two years pass.

It's a rainy night, and I'm driving in my own car somewhere over the Green Line. Suddenly, I'm ambushed. Shots ring out, some of my tires go flat, and in front of me is a barricade of stones. I slam on the brakes and my car stalls.

I see figures coming towards my car from all sides. I know what's going to happen next. They'll shoot through my non-bulletproof windshield, and then come over and fire at close range to make sure I'm dead. They have all the time in the world, and tomorrow, I'll be in the papers.

I try to start up the motor to get away, but they're already closing in on me.

One of them opens the door and throws me down onto the road, and they all start kicking me. The pain is excruciating, but I know this is only the first course. They're just having fun before they kill me.

Then a masked figure comes over. He seems to be their leader. "Enough playing around," he says. "Shoot the dog."

One of them turns me over and aims his Kalashnikov at me. Then I hear someone say, "Wait a minute."

The guy with the mask comes over, looks me in the face, and says, "Beat it everyone. I know him. He's all right."

They all run for the hills, while my rescuer stands there looking at me.

After a few moments he pulls off his mask. It's Ataf.

His eyes burn with hatred. He spits on the ground and says, "For Jalal, I'm letting you live." He gives me a good kick, and walks away.

I pinch myself. I can't believe I'm still alive. I pick myself up and start running in the direction I'd come from. Thank God, a driver stops for me, and I tell him what had happened and warn him of the ambush ahead. He whips out his cell phone and calls the police. We're told that help would soon arrive. Among other things, I'm now in need of a tow truck myself.

&#127916;   &#127916;   &#127916;

When my family and friends heard what had happened they were all in shock. Strangely, the incident was hardly mentioned in the news, maybe because there were a lot of shootings going on in the territories at that time, and my story wasn't sensational enough.

My family has been urging me for a long time to send you this story. I'm writing it to you on the anniversary of the event — a day that I now observe each year, to celebrate the miracle that happened to me.

I don't know what has become of Ataf. The only way I could find out for sure would be to ask around in his village — something that I certainly have no intention of doing. If a Jew would go into that village in the light of day, it would take a miracle for him to get out of there in one piece. And we aren't permitted to rely on miracles — certainly not just to satisfy curiosity.

One thing, though, is clear: I've had a living lesson in the meaning of the verse: "Cast your bread upon the waters, for after many days you shall find it." When you do a favor for someone without expecting something in return, in the end you'll be rewarded for it.

# One Moment of Anger

I'm full of emotion as I sit down to write this story; this is my release after a week of incredible tension.

I'm a twenty-year-old girl, and recently I've been preoccupied with *shidduchim*. A few suggestions that I was interested in have been held up, and I've been having trouble making up my mind about others. So a week before last, on *motza'ei Shabbos*, I decided to go to the Kosel and pour out my heart.

I *davened* there with a lot of *kavanah*, and then I went to the Number 2 bus stop to go home. There were an awful lot of people standing in line, and I could see I was in for a long wait.

A bus came, filled up, and left, and then another bus, and another. I waited patiently. I didn't push, but I did try to keep my place in line.

Then another bus came, and I figured I'd be able to get on that one. It was filling up fast, but I was almost at the door.

Just when I'd managed to put my foot on the step, a girl

about my age suddenly approached from the side and started squeezing in ahead of me.

"Excuse me," I said to her. "If you don't mind, there are people here who've been waiting a long time."

"I've been waiting for half an hour, too," she said.

"Really?" I said. "I didn't see you here until this moment."

She didn't answer me, and she kept her grip on the railing.

At that moment, I felt a tremendous desire to push her away and get on the bus in her place, but at the same time I didn't want to lose my temper in a moment of anger. I managed to keep a calm expression on my face, while still keeping my place on the steps.

The girl ended up getting on the bus before me, and then she turned around and signaled to me that I should get on as well. I tried, but the driver said he was full and told the girl to move further inside. "Wait a second, there's someone on the steps..." He started closing the door, so I jumped back and was left outside.

The girl made an apologetic gesture with her hands, and that made me even madder. I gave her an angry look, and under my breath I said a few words that I didn't think fit to say out loud, and if not for the fact that I was feeling so angry, I never would have said them at all. But my rage got the better of me, and the words I hissed were, "I hope you don't get home."

I was so frustrated. I got into a waiting cab, one of those shared taxis that seats about ten people for the same price as the bus. It followed the Number 2 bus route. Several minutes into the trip, we heard an explosion. It sounded very close. "It's a terror attack," the driver said.

Within minutes we could hear the ambulances coming, and then we saw them. Traffic came to a standstill, so the cab driver let us out. I started running towards the scene of the attack, but I couldn't get close because the whole area had already been cordoned off.

From where I was standing, though, I could see the bus. It was the bus I'd tried so hard to get on. I was in shock. My life had just been spared.

The next thing I thought of was that girl. What had happened to her? I'd heard the tremendous boom and the screams, and I knew she might very well be lying there... and then I remembered the terrible words I'd let out of my mouth.

I went home, stunned and confused. I couldn't think of anything but that girl. My parents were terrified; when I walked in the door, they hugged me as if I'd just returned from the next world. "You could have been on that bus," they said.

Chewing my nails, I followed the news reports. I kept picturing that girl in my mind. I hated myself for being angry at her and remembered that, after all, she'd tried to help me get on the bus. I remembered how cynical I'd been towards her. And most of all, I remembered what I'd said under my breath, and felt as if everything that happened was my fault. A person says a lot of things without thinking. Sometimes, those careless words become very meaningful.

First thing the next morning, I scanned the newspaper, trying to find out who'd been killed or injured. The reports said there were a few young girls among the dead, but there were no pictures.

A day or two later, the names came out in the news. But I didn't know the girl's name, and there were still no pictures.

I didn't tell anyone about what had happened. I had a terrible feeling inside, but I was afraid to talk about it. My parents noticed that something was wrong with me, and naturally, they figured it had something to do with the bombing. They thought I might be suffering from shock, and suggested I go see a doctor.

I couldn't sleep at night. I kept picturing her face, and its gentle expression when she signaled to me to get on the bus, and afterwards when she spoke to the driver and then gave me an apologetic look. And I remembered what I'd given her in return for her trouble — an angry look and a few unspeakable words. I wondered if she had read my lips. Had she seen how angry I was? I imagined her looking down from the upper world and saying, "It was all because of you."

The whole business was burdening my heart like a ton of bricks. I'd never thought I would feel so much regret for saying a few words.

A week went by like that. The following Tuesday I decided to go to the Kosel, to *daven* and to ask that girl for *mechilah*. I leaned on the stones and cried like I've never cried before in my life. I begged forgiveness from the girl and from Hashem, because it might have been my curse that brought about the disaster.

On the one hand, I tried to convince myself that if something was decreed in Heaven, a few words from me wouldn't make a difference one way or the other, but on the other hand, I'd once learned that there's such a thing as an *eis ratzon*, a time when blessings and curses are fulfilled. Maybe it had been an *eis ratzon* that *motza'ei Shabbos*, and maybe if I'd said something good, instead of what I'd said, the whole tragedy could have been prevented.

The burden on my conscience was indescribable. There, by the Kosel stones, I let it all out.

I dried my tears and walked slowly back to the bus stop. Every step reminded me of the terrible events of the week before.

I stood quietly waiting for the bus, promising myself not to push ahead, and certainly not to get into a disagreement with anyone. The bus pulled up and as I gently made my way forward, I glanced behind me. And there she was.

She was standing to the side of the bus stop, saying *Tehillim* fervently.

I left the line of people boarding the bus and ran over to her. I grabbed her arm feverishly and asked, "Do you remember me."

She looked at me in amazement.

"I don't believe it," she murmured. "So you're alive and well?"

"You're asking about me?!" I practically yelled. "I'm asking the same thing about you!"

"I don't believe it," she repeated. "I was afraid something happened to you. Don't ask what I've been going through all week. I was so afraid you were one of the…"

She looked so relieved and happy. I'm sure I looked the same.

"But why were you afraid something happened to me?" I asked her. "You saw with your own eyes that I didn't get on that bus."

"What?" she said, her eyes popping wide open. "You mean the bus I was on was the one that…"

Now I was completely confused. As a general rule, when people are riding on buses that explode, they don't forget it so easily. Maybe she'd been struck with amnesia or something?

"I don't understand," I said. "I was in a taxi right behind

160

your bus, and I saw what happened. How could you not know about it?"

"Oh..." she said. "Now I see. You thought I was still on the bus. Actually, I got off at the first stop because I'd forgotten my *Tehillim* at the Kosel. I walked back, found my *Tehillim*, and waited for another bus. Afterwards I heard about the bombing, and right away I thought of you. I thought that since I'd gotten on the bus ahead of you, you were forced to wait for the next bus, and according to my calculations, *that* was the bus that exploded.

"I've been feeling so horribly guilty, I can't tell you," she said. "For more than a week I've hardly slept or eaten. Today, I decided to come to the Kosel and *daven....*" She paused, because the next words she had in mind were, "for your departed soul."

"So you were saved by the *sefer Tehillim* you left behind — and you didn't even know it!" I said.

Suddenly, it all sank in. "I can't believe it," she said. "I almost got killed! I could have died that night, but I was saved."

Then I told her what kind of torment I'd been going through since then. I admitted that I'd said something I shouldn't have and told her how I'd been blaming myself for what had happened.

We sat on a bench and talked for about two hours. At the end of our conversation we decided that we have to publicize our story.

We live our lives, and we don't realize that everything we say and do is of fateful significance. My friend, the girl who got on the bus instead of me, saved me from that explosion. I, unlike her, hadn't left any *Tehillim* behind, and I would have stayed on the bus — until the end. She was annoyed with herself for being forgetful, and she grumbled inwardly about having to trudge all the way back to the Kosel on foot, never realizing that by forgetting the *Tehillim*, she had saved her own life.

Hashem is the One Who keeps this world turning and co-ordinates all earthly events, and we have no idea how everything really works.

But the main thing for us to learn here is the importance of the words we speak. As *Chazal* said, "A covenant is made with the lips"; in other words, we must be careful what we say, because it might come true. That's how powerful words are.

# A Match Made in Heaven

My story took place more than ten years ago.

I come from a well-respected family, and have always been considered to be one of the best *bachurim* in the prestigious yeshivos where I studied. So when I reached marriageable age, I was highly sought-after as a prospective *chasan*.

As for me, of course I wanted a girl who was intelligent and had good *middos*, but beyond that I had no specific demands.

However, my parents had a few demands on my behalf. They felt that I had real potential to become a great *talmid chacham* and they wanted to ensure that I would be able to learn for many years without financial worries. Today, especially in Eretz Yisrael where we live, it is common for the parents to buy their children an apartment, so that the son/son-in-law will be able to stay in *kollel* for as long as possible. In many circles, the parents go half-and-half. By us, it's customary that the girl's side buys the apartment. My parents felt that a boy of my caliber shouldn't settle for less.

After we had rejected a few suggestions, someone mentioned the name of a very good girl. We made inquiries and she met my parents' criteria.

From the first moment I met her, I immediately sensed that she was right for me. She had all the qualities I was looking for. I knew this was the girl my parents and I had been seeking.

We met three times and everything went smoothly. After each date we let the *shadchan* know that we were interested in meeting again, and she set up yet another date.

On our fifth date, as we were strolling down the street, I suddenly stopped short. Facing her, I said that I thought she was my true *zivug* and asked her if she felt the same way. Impulsively, I asked her to marry me right then and there. She nodded, very emotional. A moment after the importance of this revelation sunk in, we hurried to a public phone to call our parents.

Both sets of parents were delighted. That was on a Sunday. They arranged to meet each other on Tuesday night in the girl's parents' home in order to settle the financial issues.

Very excited, I returned to yeshivah and confided to my best friends that I had proposed and that hopefully I'd be celebrating a *vort* in two days' time.

On the fateful day, my parents and I went to the girl's house. After brief introductions, our parents "banished" us from the house so they could "argue in peace." That's how my father put it. He had no idea how true his prediction would be.

We took a cab to a nearby hotel and sat in the lobby and talked. After about a half an hour, I suggested we call her house and ask if everything had been settled.

We called and her parents said we should come back as soon as possible.

We went outside and flagged down a cab. On the way, we felt as if we were already officially engaged. We knew that as soon as we arrived, we'd drink *l'chaim* and shortly thereafter our friends would burst into the house singing "*Kol sason v'kol simchah.*"

We arrived.

As soon as I saw my parents' faces, I knew something was wrong. My father was the first to speak. "We have a problem," he said. "The *shadchan* misled us. We need to think the matter over very carefully."

We waited for him to go on, but my parents merely rose, shook hands with the girl's parents and told me, "Let's go."

"Wait a minute," I said. "What's going on?"

"We'll explain at home," my parents replied.

I wanted to talk to the girl but she was just as shocked as I was. We looked at each other. She was pale; I imagine I was too.

☙        ☙        ☙

We were still in the street when my father began venting. "That's a real chutzpah, what that *shadchan* did," he said. "How could she have fooled us like that?"

When he saw how confused I looked, he explained, "The *shadchan* told us that the girl's side would be willing to pay for an apartment. During the first five minutes of our meeting we realized there had been a misunderstanding. The girl's family cannot afford to buy even a tenth of an apartment, let alone a whole one. They can pay for half the expenses of a very simple wedding. They told me that they'd have to take a loan just to buy you a gold watch! We were tricked, son."

I was silent. I felt as if my whole world was falling apart. "We were tricked," my father was saying again. "The *shadchan* put a fast one over on us." My mind was reeling.

"It's a good thing we discovered it in time," I heard my mother say, and I opened my mouth for the first time since we'd left the girl's house.

"It's not exactly 'in time,'" I said. "I made a commitment to that girl."

"Don't worry about," my father said. "Someone mentioned an excellent suggestion, one that we should have looked into first. It can't be helped; no one said *shidduchim* were a picnic."

"But Abba, maybe you didn't pay attention to what I said. I made a commitment to this girl."

"Nonsense," my father said dismissively. "These things happen all the time. As long as there was no *vort*, there's no significance to what either of you told the other."

It seemed as though whatever I said made no impression on him. I understood that there was nothing to talk about. The *shidduch* was history.

📧    📧    📧

I don't know why, but even though I was brokenhearted about what had happened, I didn't make much of an effort to revive that *shidduch*. Looking back, I know I didn't express to my parents the sense of loss I felt. Maybe it was because I had always been an obedient son and never expressed an opinion that conflicted with theirs. I just assumed that they had my own best interests at heart — I still think so, by the way — but foolishly, I didn't tell them how hard the situation was for me.

Two weeks later, I began dating again. I went out with a few girls and then I met one girl from a good family who seemed like a good match. There was no reason not to go ahead. She, too, was interested right from the start, and it wasn't long before we agreed to marry.

Our parents got together the following evening. To my surprise, it was a very brief meeting. I learned that my parents had taken no chances this time. Without my knowledge, they had met with the *kallah*'s parents immediately after our first date. They demanded and received all the commitments they wanted — and they were very sizeable commitments. All that was left to do was drink *l'chaim* — and that's what we did.

My *vort/tenayim* was a very elegant affair. We were both very popular and dozens, if not hundreds, of our respective friends attended. The happiness I felt made me forget the anguish and misery I had experienced not that long before.

My engagement period was wonderful. My *kallah*'s family received me warmly and was very proud of me. My fiancée was sweet and intelligent, and everything seemed like a dream.

The wedding was beautiful, and immediately thereafter we moved into the new apartment my wife's parents had purchased for us.

Now began a period that was as bad as it was brief. From the second day of the marriage, we began to fight. Actually, I shouldn't say *we* began to fight. She would pick a fight with me, I would apologize, and she wouldn't forgive me until the next fight.

She didn't approve of a single thing I did — not the way I ate, not the way I spoke, not the way I talked, and not even the way I slept.

When the week of *Sheva Berachos* was over, real life began — except it wasn't life; it was a prolonged nightmare. My wife was incomparably critical and cynical.

Personally, I had no complaints about her. She cooked,

did the laundry and kept the house perfectly neat and clean. Maybe that was the problem: She was too perfect in all areas — except for her *middos*, which left much to be desired. But I didn't realize that at the time.

Until my marriage, I thought that I, too, was pretty much perfect, but she informed me that it wasn't so at all. She told me that I was an ill-mannered boor, awkward and lazy. She used harsh words and shattered my spirit.

But on the outside — all was sweetness and light. No one knew a thing.

I didn't say a word to anyone. I had no idea that I was enduring a terrible experience. I knew only one thing: I wasn't happy. I told myself that I really wasn't up to par and had to change in order to be worthy of the woman who had agreed to marry me. It didn't occur to me to question her accusations. It certainly never entered my mind that perhaps it hadn't been a good idea to marry her.

It was she who stopped the torture. Two months after my marriage, I arrived home to find the house neat as a pin. One glance was enough to tell me that she had taken all her things, leaving me with a neatly made bed, my clothing in the closet and a small note telling me that she had left. I could contact her parents for details.

✎        ✎        ✎

I called my parents and told them what had happened. I felt utterly humiliated. I began to cry and apologize. I told them I was willing to do whatever she wanted.

My father called her parents and heard from them the litany of complaints she had hurled at me over the past two months.

My parents were absolutely stunned. They asked me if what she claimed was true, and I didn't know how to answer.

"You know me," I said. "You know how I eat, walk and talk. I haven't changed. She thinks I'm all wrong and she made sure to let me know it. The truth is that I've almost come to believe it, too. If you also think she's right, maybe I should go for counseling."

Luckily for me, my parents were smarter than that. They sat me down and told me that they saw nothing wrong with anything I did. On the contrary, they thought I was a kind and gentle soul.

They encouraged me to tell them about what had transpired during the past two months. For the first time, I told all. When I was done, my parents sat opposite me and wept. I had never seen them like that before.

"Listen to me, my dear son," my mother said, "you married a difficult woman with very poor *middos*. You're lucky she decided to leave you, because I doubt we would have ever learned of your suffering otherwise. She could have wrecked you emotionally."

For the next few days, my parents spoke to me everyday, reassuring me, and slowly restored my confidence that it wasn't I who was at fault. At first, I thought they were just trying to make me feel better, but a brief conversation with my father, who is a very candid person and has no problem delivering criticism when it's warranted, convinced me that wasn't the case.

"Believe me, son," he said. "If I thought the problem was with you, I would sit you down and point out where you had gone wrong. But after all that's happened, I made some additional inquiries about her. Rest assured, there is nothing wrong with you. You were burned. You have to believe what I'm telling you."

☙      ☙      ☙

The *get* was arranged very quickly after a series of negotiations in *beis din*.

It was an experience I don't wish on anyone, especially not as the party on the receiving end of the *get*. I stood there wracked with humiliation and pain. She stood there proudly and confidently as she accepted the *get*.

My parents reached an agreement with her parents regarding the *get* and I, a twenty-one-year-old young man, found myself newly divorced. My glorious past as a *yeshivah bachur* with a shining reputation was obliterated in the face of my new status as an object of pity.

I was in a state of terrible despair. I barely managed to drag myself out of bed in the morning to *daven* and learn. I had no strength to go on. The humiliation I had endured over the past two months had wreaked havoc on me.

Two weeks after the divorce, my parents received a call from the *shadchan*, the same one my parents had been angry with for "tricking" them. She wanted to suggest a *shidduch*: the same girl I had very nearly gotten engaged to, the one who my parents had rejected because her family wasn't wealthy enough.

Apparently, the girl knew I was divorced and didn't care. She still wanted to marry me. Her parents tried to dissuade her and even took her to one of the *gedolei hador* to convince her to drop the idea. To their surprise, the *gadol* told them that I was their daughter's true *zivug* and advised them to agree to their daughter's request immediately.

My parents were delighted that someone was interested in me — an excellent, unmarried girl to boot. They wasted no time in giving the *shadchan* a positive response.

We met — again. It's hard for me to describe that meeting. At first, I couldn't bring myself to look her in the face, but she very wisely began to chat about this and that, as if this was our sixth date, as if half a year hadn't destroyed everything we had built, as if I hadn't preferred another girl over her just because her parents didn't have money. She chatted with me about her teaching job, her brother's new baby daughter and her deliberation over whether or not to accept a new position she'd been offered.

We chatted lightly for a while until there was a sudden lull in our conversation.

And then I heard myself say, "I have something that I must tell you."

Silence.

"I'm so sorry," I said, bursting into uncontrollable sobs. At first, she tried to hold back her own tears, but then she joined me.

We spoke for a long time and then once again promised each other that we would marry.

Ten years have passed since then. I'm married and the father of five children. I'm as happy as a man could be. My wife is the kind of woman *Eishes Chayil* was written for.

And I heard that my divorcée remarried — more than once.

There's a reason I decided to tell my personal story. I would like other people to benefit from it.

My story cries out to each and every person, be it a *bachur* on the brink of getting engaged or the parent of a child in "the *parashah*": If a couple has reached the decision that they are compatible, it is forbidden to allow a trivial matter — certainly not money — to come between them. And if money is of such critical importance — make sure that aspect is discussed and settled before the couple meets.

To newlyweds who read my story, I call for a bit of patience and lots of good *middos*. You can't change your spouse in a quarter of an hour, half a year or even ten years. Sometimes, it's impossible to effect any change, ever. In any case, verbal insults certainly accomplish nothing. Be patient; don't ruin your lives with your own hands.

To people who were forced to divorce, I say this: Do not despair. I still clearly recall those awful two weeks after my divorce. More than once I entertained thoughts I don't care to detail here. That's how humiliated and outcast I felt. And then, all of a sudden, my future was bright again and my life filled with joy. Remember that and hope for the best.

In conclusion, I'd like to offer a few words of gratitude to my dear wife, who forgave the insult to her pride and recognized that we were truly a match made in Heaven!

# *Public Relations*

I've read the first two volumes of the *People Speak* series, and I feel a need to write down this story of mine.

It isn't about me; it's about a man who was a classmate of mine some thirty years ago. We were classmates for only about a year and a half, from the time my family moved to that town until we left.

Whenever we had a test at school, this boy would send notes around to the whole class, wishing us all success on the exam. I remember it as clearly as if it happened today. It was an unusual thing for a boy to do, but most of the kids didn't make fun of this initiative of his, and I'll explain why in a moment. They would read the notes, fold them up, and put them in their shirt pockets.

He was really such a caring person, that boy. He used to remember the birthdays of every kid in the class. And if he didn't know the date, he would take the trouble to find out. Whenever it was boy's birthday, he would give him a flower that he picked from the garden in front of the school, along with a note saying "*Mazal tov* on your birthday," and a few personal remarks. It was an odd thing to do, but the kids really looked forward to it.

I remember one time when a kid got upset because he thought his birthday had been forgotten. Just then the boy took a rumpled flower out of his pocket, with a note attached to it, and said to the kid, "How could you think I'd forget you? I was just waiting for class to be over."

Looking back on all this thirty years later, I recall images of that boy and I realize that it was those two practices that protected him from being teased. You see, he was a chubby kid and had a high-pitched, squeaky voice. Boys can be cruel — and that class was a good example. But instead of teasing him about these things, they left him alone.

Why? That's just the way it was.

I think that even though some of the boys would laugh at him behind his back because of these odd gestures of his, deep inside they wanted that attention, or at least, nobody wanted to be excluded and *not* get a flower on his birthday or a good-luck note before a test. The boys wanted to stay on his good side, and they avoided hurting him, if only to assure themselves of those special attentions.

After a year and a half, as I said, I left that school. Over the years I forgot those classmates, including the chubby boy with his funny customs.

Not too long ago, I happened to be present at a press conference where a well-known public-relations man was speaking. I was sitting in the back of the room and at first I only heard him talking. Every so often his voice would crack, in a squeaky sort of way, and that brought back memories of my classmate. When I moved forward to get a better look at the speaker, I was sure that this was the boy I'd known back in my schooldays. He had a pretty common name, so until that point I hadn't made the connection.

I conducted a little investigation, which wasn't difficult at all. Since he was a famous man, it was easy to get information about him. It turned out that he's the biggest public relations man in the country, a person who all the big corporations hire to explain their positions, knowing that he'll put them in the best possible light.

Public relations as a profession consists mainly of acting as a mediator between the press and people who either want to advance their interests through the media or want to avoid getting bad press. For that, you need a person who knows how to win the reporters over, so that they'll portray the PR man's clients in the best possible way. Anyone who knows what journalists are like will realize how hard a job it is.

Asking around about him, I discovered that he still adheres to those practices of his, that we as students found so odd. He knows the birthdays of thousands of the most influential people in the country: politicians, journalists, corporate heads, and senior army officials. He sends a bouquet of flowers, together with a personal greeting, to every single one of them. He also keeps abreast of family events in their lives — births, bar mitzvahs, weddings, and on the other side, times of mourning or trouble. He calls them up to say *mazal tov* or to give words of encouragement or sympathy.

When I knew him as a boy, he had braces on his teeth, but now he has a thousand-watt smile — a smile so genuine that it makes you want to smile right back. The Gemara in *Maseches Kesuvos* says, "One who whitens his teeth to his fellow man is better than one who gives him a drink of milk." In other words, a smile and a good word do more for a person than any material gift.

This man is able to melt the hearts of the most hardened

journalists. He succeeds in causing them not to want to disappoint him. Over the years, he's expanded his operations, and he also negotiates mergers and deals between business moguls.

Today, he's considered a member of Israel's wealthy class, but that's only a minor detail compared to the influence he has on important figures and the decisions they make.

What's interesting about this whole story is that the journalists know perfectly well how he works his magic. They write about him admiringly and sometimes critically, but they acknowledge that they can't resist his charm.

All this leads to very important conclusions: Evidently, people love to get attention and compliments. Of course, they won't necessarily admit it; they'll even fend off compliments with a wave of the hand. But the compliment will win them over nonetheless, and its influence will show in their actions.

The second conclusion is that it appears that most people aren't capable of really being nice to others, of truly caring deeply for their fellow man.

Where do I get that idea from?

From the fact that everybody knows what the man's methods are, and despite that, not a single person in the country is applying them — and this, in a country where every good idea is immediately copied by others.

It seems that this is an idea that can't be copied. Either it's a natural part of your makeup or it's not.

Giving attention to others is a hard task, because it means you have to think about somebody else besides yourself. Most people have difficulty doing that even when it comes to their relatives, their spouse, their children and their friends. So how can they remember someone outside of their immediate circle?

I think that my classmate was truly a special person, blessed with exceptional *middos*. He wasn't putting on an act. You can't fool people when it comes to these things. He simply took his greatest personality trait — sincere interest in others — and turned it into a key to success.

Personally, I've taken this man as an example, and I've started keeping track of birthdays, special occasions, and even exams or other crucial events in the lives of my family and acquaintances.

I've discovered how hard it is to check an appointment book every day and see whose birthday it is, and it's even harder to pick up the phone and give him my best wishes. To show this level of interest and caring certainly demands time and patience.

It's hard, but on the other hand, it gives a lot of satisfaction not only to the person you're showing an interest in, but also to yourself.

Don't worry; I'm not planning to go into public relations. I have a good, steady job already. But without a doubt, my re-encounter with the squeaky-voiced boy I knew in school thirty years ago, has changed my life for the better.

# Lifesaver

O ur story occurred many years ago. But despite the time that has elapsed, it's as fresh in my mind as if it happened yesterday. Every time we see our daughters, Bracha and Miri, we're reminded of the miracle we merited.

We had driven up to the northern part of Israel, arriving in Tiberias in the afternoon. My husband went to *daven Minchah* at the grave of Rabbi Meir Ba'al HaNes and my daughters and I went to sit on the rocks near Lake Kinneret and enjoy the view while we waited for him to return.

The girls asked if they could wade into in the lake a bit to cool off. I was a little hesitant since neither of them knew how to swim, but I gave them permission to go on in. I sat perched on a large rock near the water and watched as they removed their shoes and socks, and started splashing around in the water.

After a while, they waded a bit further into the water. I immediately called out to them not to go in any deeper but apparently they didn't hear me.

Suddenly, I saw Bracha, my older daughter, trip and fall into the water.

At first, my younger daughter laughed, and I chuckled, too, but then I saw Bracha being swept out further into the lake. I jump up and instinctively ran towards the water to rescue her when I remembered that I myself didn't know how to swim. So I turned around and ran up to the main road and tried to flag down a passing car.

The first few cars drove right by me. By this time I was so frantic that I stepped into the middle of the road, waving my arms around wildly. Drivers swerved to avoid me and honked their horns as if I were a crazy woman.

Just then an elegant car pulled to a stop. A man in a suit and tie got out and asked what was wrong. I told him my daughter was drowning.

He didn't think twice. Throwing off his suit jacket, he ran to the rocks. "Be careful," his wife called after him. "Don't forget you're recovering from a heart attack!"

He leapt over the rocks and dove into the water.

He swam a bit and fished a child out of the water. I immediately saw that it was Miri and not Bracha. Apparently, Miri had tried to save Bracha and had also been swept out to deeper water.

"Save Bracha!" I screamed to him. He didn't understand what I was saying. A few passersby who had come over to try to help began shouting, "There's another girl in the water!"

The man managed to pull Miri to shallow water, and although she was coughing terribly, she appeared to be relatively unharmed.

The man quickly dove back into the water again to find Bracha.

The truth is that, at that point, I had despaired. I saw no

sign of my daughter. I feared that she had sunk all the way to the bottom of the lake. I was watching the man intently as he frantically swam this way and that, trying to find my daughter. Suddenly he dove down under the water and resurfaced a moment or two later holding my daughter under his arm.

As he swam towards shore with my daughter in tow, I noticed that her head was still inside the water.

"Her head's in the water!" I shouted.

"Pick up her head so she can breathe!" the other people called out to Bracha's rescuer.

He lifted her head and when I saw her, I was sure that she was no longer alive. Her face was nearly black.

He placed her on the shore and said, "I'm sorry, but I think she's dead." His face was pale. I was afraid he really was going to have a heart attack.

Just then a man came running down the beach. He had seen what had happened and realized that he could help. "I know first-aid," he called out, and wasted no time pushing his way through the crowd that had now gathered. He crouched down next to Bracha and began administering CPR.

His name was Hatib, and he was a resident of a nearby Arab village.

Hatib did his best to breathe life into my daughter while I prayed and wept. I saw my daughter in a lifeless body. I pleaded with Hashem that in the merit of Rabbi Meir Ba'al HaNes a miracle should occur and my daughter should live.

The crowd seemed to have given up hope, but Hatib kept working. Suddenly, Bracha began to cough and water streamed from her mouth. That was the first sign of life.

Just then, an ambulance arrived.

I rode with Bracha to a nearby hospital. From there we were transferred to Rambam Hospital in Haifa. The doctors there despaired of saving Bracha's life. They told me that someone who had been in the water for so long had very little chance for survival. And even if she were by some miracle to survive, they said, she would be a vegetable due to the damage that her brain had surely sustained.

However, in middle of the night, Bracha showed signs of independent breathing. The doctors scanned her brain and were flabbergasted to see that her brain activity was normal. "She'll be okay," they told me. "It's a miracle."

Two days later, we left the hospital with our daughter in perfect health.

We stopped off at the *kever* of Rabbi Meir Ba'al HaNes to express our gratitude to Hashem for the miracle He had performed for us, and then we returned home.

All during that time, we had been in touch with the man who had saved Bracha. His name was Yitzchak Barzilai and he was an attorney who lived in Ramat Hasharon. He kept calling to inquire how Bracha was doing. When he heard she was out of danger, he cried out with joy. "I knew it," he exclaimed with emotion.

🎬   🎬   🎬

Two weeks later, we held a *seudas hoda'ah* to express our gratitude to Hashem for sparing Bracha's life. Of course, we wanted to invite both the lawyer and Hatib, the Arab who had performed CPR. We had Mr. Barzilai's number, but we couldn't locate Hatib.

At the celebration, which was very moving, Yitzchak Barzilai told his story, which proved to be no less amazing than Bracha's rescue miracle.

"On the day that Bracha, here, almost drowned," he related, "my wife and I had set out from home to spend a few weeks at our vacation home in a small village just north of

Tiberias. We left early in the morning, because along the way I was scheduled to stop for a quick business meeting in one of the hotels in Tiberias. When the meeting was over, the hotel manager offered me a cup of coffee and something to eat, but I told my wife I wanted to leave right away.

"'Let's stay for another few minutes,' she cajoled me.

"But I insisted on leaving. I was eager to get to our vacation home. We hadn't been there in quite some time. My wife tried to convince me to stay longer, but I was already on my way out of the hotel.

"I have to digress for a moment to tell you that I have always been an excellent swimmer, but I hadn't been near a pool since I suffered a heart attack last year. The previous day, I suddenly decided I wanted to go swimming. My wife objected, concerned that it would prove too strenuous for me, but I told her I'd be okay and went swimming at our local pool. I spent two hours doing laps.

"When I returned home, my wife was really upset. She felt that I was being reckless. 'It isn't worth risking your life just to satisfy a passing whim,' she told me.

"Neither of us knew at that point that the One Above had put the idea in my head in order to be able to *save* a life.

"So as we drove down the road that ran along the lake, my wife eyed the water and said to me, half in jest but really with annoyance: 'Are you planning another swimming marathon for today?'

"Before I could think how to respond to my wife's comment, I suddenly saw an Orthodox woman standing in middle of the road, screaming and waving her arms. No one was stopping for her. 'Save my daughter!' she was screaming. 'Save my daughter!'

"I stopped the car. 'Be careful,' my wife warned. 'Don't forget you're recovering from a heart attack!' But I was already on my way down, leaping over the slippery rocks. I immediately saw a little girl in the water. I dove inside and pulled her out. When I got to the shore, the people crowding there shouted, 'There's another girl in the water.'

"I didn't see another girl. I began to dive and search. Suddenly, I noticed a white spot a few yards away from me. I swam over there and dove down. The water was only about six-feet deep. I saw a girl lying motionless on the bottom of the lake. I pulled her up to the surface and began to swim as fast as I could.

"'Lift her head!' the crowd shouted to me. 'Her head's still in the water!'

"When I reached the shore, I staggered out of the water and gently set the girl down in the sand.

"My wife was trying her best to help; she told me that she had already called for an ambulance.

"That's when the young Arab man showed up and began to administer first-aid. I hoped dearly that his efforts would succeed in reviving her, but at the same time, I doubted they would. And then water began streaming from her mouth. An ambulance arrived and she was taken to the hospital.

"I was very shaken up, but we continued on to our vacation home.

"That night, I was supposed to meet friends at the Jordan River for a party. On the way over there, at about 11:00, I told my wife I needed some fresh air. Although I'm not at all religious, I left my car, climbed a hill on the side of the road, and began to talk to God.

"I felt terrible that I hadn't noticed that the girl's head was still in the water when I first began swimming back to shore with her. 'You know I'm a good swimmer,' I said, addressing the Heavens. 'You sent me there to save her. Please, God,' I pleaded, 'make her live.' I felt like a lawyer pleading before the greatest Judge in the world about an issue of life or death. And, in fact, that was really the case.

"When I was finished, I returned to my car and we continued on our way to meet our friends, but it was no longer a regular night for me. At some point, I left the party and called the hospital. They told me the girl was in critical condition.

"I despaired.

"In the morning, I called again and they told me that a short while after I'd called, the girl had come to and was now in the recovery room.

"I want to tell you something. My decision to get back into shape for swimming the previous night and my arrival at the spot where Bracha was drowning at just the right time were undoubtedly Divine Supervision at work, as was Hatib's arrival at the scene. Both of us were sent by Heaven to save both Miri and Bracha."

And Mr. Barzilai sat down.

But the story is still not over.

When the attorney concluded his speech, we gave him a gift: a framed bas-relief picture of Chassidim sitting around a table that held lit candles. Mr. Barzilai tore the wrapping paper and blanched as soon as he saw the picture.

He showed it to his wife, who gave a little yelp and began to cry.

We couldn't imagine what had happened. We certainly hadn't expected such a reaction from his wife, who had struck us as a very quiet woman.

It took the attorney a few minutes to recover, but then he took the microphone again and said, "This cannot possibly be a coincidence. My father, may he rest in peace, made just such a bas relief during the final days of his life as part of the occupational therapy program he participated in at the nursing home where he was living."

He fell silent for a minute and then added, "You won't believe this, but we hung my father's bas relief on the wall in the bedroom of our vacation home. The real reason I was so eager to get there in a hurry was that I had been thinking about that picture. I missed it and wanted to see it again."

Well, that's the story; every word is true.

Unfortunately, Hatib disappeared before we managed to thank him properly or hear his story. Had he not been passing by, Bracha would surely have died. We feel certain that his testimony would also underscore the marvelous *hash-gachah pratis* we merited that day and further augment *kevod Shamayim.*

# *Return to Sender*

It is with great emotion that I write these words. Although my name won't be publicized, many people may identify me through my story. Still, it is a story I feel must be told.

I grew up as a normal child, one of five siblings. Nothing in my life was unusual until I reached the age of twelve. At that time I began to feel terribly weak and experienced a few fainting spells. Intensive testing led to devastating news: I had cancer.

My life changed at once. Nothing was the same anymore. Instead of going to school, I was in the hospital; instead of socializing with my classmates, I spoke to my roommates and the other kids in the oncology ward; instead of playing all day, I was subjected to test after test without letup; instead of feeling fine, I felt positively awful.

Three months after I was hospitalized, I learned that I would participate in a week-long Ezer Mizion camp. To be perfectly honest, the word "camp" did not excite me. I had grown up so much in the past three months that it sounded to me like kindergarten. I didn't feel like participating in anything. I wanted to be left alone in my bed, in my room.

But my parents insisted on taking me to the camp.

I learned very quickly that it was not an ordinary camp; it was nothing like any of the ones I had ever attended before. I'm not talking about the trips, shows and attractions. I'm not dismissing them, either, of course, but it was something else that made that camp truly special.

We were approximately a hundred sick kids of various ages and each of us was accompanied by family members. That in itself was wonderful. I was finally able to spend time with my brothers and sisters in a setting other than the hospital. I could pretend I was a guest in a hotel!

But it was my counselor who really boosted my inner strength and willpower to get better.

In camps like this one, there are no bunks. Every child is assigned a counselor. My counselor's name was Refael. He was an angel, as his name indicates.

I cannot begin to describe the *ko'ach* that this special *bachur* gave me. He didn't try to convince me that I was having a great time and that other kids ought to be jealous of me. But he didn't allow me to feel like a *nebach* case either. He just leveled with me and persuaded me to open up to him. I felt safe with him.

He was only about sixteen years old, but he was as wise as a man of thirty. He was sensitive and kind but also smart and authoritative.

I became very close to him and we both knew that this was a bond for life. And that's exactly what happened. We maintained steady contact throughout the year through telephone calls and visits. Refael went though all my treatments together with me, helping me cope with the hair loss, the desperate longing for remission, the disappointment, additional treatment, additional disappointments and hopes.

He also learned with me and organized other *chavrusas* to learn with me, as well, so I wouldn't lag behind in my learning. He infused me with physical, emotional and spiritual life.

✍ ✍ ✍

That year, I celebrated my bar mitzvah, though "celebrated" might not be the right word. It was a celebration rife with emotion and tears, with hopes and fears. It was the type of bar mitzvah you might expect for a boy whose time on earth might end at any time.

A year passed and it was time for the Ezer Mizion camp again. I made sure to tell the camp director in advance whom I wanted for my counselor. The look in his eyes told me my request was completely superfluous.

Once again, Refael and I were together for a week. This time, we weren't counselor and camper but rather two friends having a ball together. Those were wonderful days that made me forget the pain and suffering that were my constant lot.

I only participated in Ezer Mizion's camp twice. The following year, the treatment was finally effective. I recovered completely and went back to school. I didn't have an easy time of it, but because I'd continued learning the entire time — with Refael as well as others — I did fairly well in eighth grade and then continued on to yeshivah.

✍ ✍ ✍

Another four years passed. I celebrated my eighteenth birthday. Refael turned twenty-two and began going out on *shidduchim*. It was almost as if we'd forgotten all about the fact that I'd once been ill. We were no longer involved with Ezer Mizion's camp — maybe because we wanted to forget what I had been through or maybe because we just didn't have time.

188

And then the worst possible thing happened. Refael was diagnosed with cancer.

That dreaded disease returned to my life with a vicious blow through the back door.

Suddenly, our positions were reversed. Strong, confident Refael became a ghostly shadow and I sat with him, spoke with him, and accompanied him day and night — in the same hospital, the same ward, practically the same room.

It occurred to me then that Hashem must be testing us and that we should look at the situation from a novel angle: perhaps it had been decreed that both of us would get sick and Hashem had arranged for us to meet so that we'd be able to strengthen each other.

Throughout the year, I visited Refael in the hospital at every available opportunity. I sat at his side, spoke to him, learned with him and arranged *chavrusas* hoping that he'd be so preoccupied it would help him not to dwell on his pain.

One evening, I suggested to Refael that we start writing letters to each other because I lived in Yerushalayim and he was hospitalized near Tel Aviv.

"No way," he said to me, only half-joking. "I'm not writing to you."

"What do you mean?" I asked, hurt. "You have a problem writing to me?"

"Yes," he replied. "When you were sick, I wrote you a long and emotional letter that made me cry even as I wrote it. It was so personal that I deliberated whether or not to give it to you. In the end I decided that it was something that I had to share with you."

"So...?" I asked.

"So... you tell me," Refael said. "I never got a response to that letter. You never said a word about it. It was as if it had never been written. I understood that you felt uncomfortable with very personal letters and I was sorry I had written it."

"I don't know about any such letter," I told him.

"What do you mean you don't know about that letter? I gave it to you in your hands."

"When was this?"

"After your transplant, when you had finished your isolation period, before they transferred you back to the regular ward."

As soon as he said the word "isolation," I understood. "I know what happened to your letter."

"Great," Refael said with annoyance, "but that doesn't answer why you never even acknowledged that letter."

"Oh, but it does," I said. "It's possible that your letter is still in isolation."

"What?"

"When you said the word 'isolation,' I remembered. You gave me the letter when I was weak and disoriented. I understood that it was something personal and I tried to think where I could hide it so no one would see it and possibly read it. I looked around and I noticed that the wall was covered with intricately designed tin beams, just like you see here in this room. I stuck the letter in there. Then I went to sleep and forgot all about it."

🎬    🎬    🎬

I approached the head nurse and pointed to the isolation room where I had spent some time years earlier. I inquired if anyone was there now.

When she told me that the room was empty, I asked her if I might go in for a moment because I'd forgotten something there.

After she gave me permission, I entered the room. A brief glance was all I needed to remember precisely in which beam

I had placed the letter. I bent down, moved the beam slightly away from its place — and the letter, still sealed in its envelope, fell into my hands like a ripe fruit.

I returned to the room, and showed Refael the letter. I opened it up and began to read — to read and to cry. The letter was filled with inspiring words of *chizuk*, words that expressed how badly he wanted me to be healthy and how strongly he believed that I still had a wonderful life ahead of me.

When I finished reading the letter for the second time, I took a pen, and drew a line through my name at the top of the letter and replaced it with Refael's. Then I scratched out his signature at the end of the letter and signed my name. I placed the letter back in the envelope and told him, "I want you to read the letter. True, I didn't write it, but I agree with every word that's written here as if I had written it to you."

He began to read and to cry. Even though he had written the letter, everything was so different now. It was as if I had taken his words and returned them to him in my name.

At that moment I knew that such a story doesn't just "happen." The letter underscored the fact that *Hakadosh Baruch Hu* had prepared a cure for Refael and for me before He sent the affliction. That letter — that Refael had written for me so long ago — had been preserved for him, to give him encouragement in his time of need.

# *Ears to Hear*

I'm the Yerushalmi *Yid* whose letters you've already printed a few times in the past. I don't mean to pressure you to print this letter, too, although my wife says this is the type of story you don't hear too often.

The story begins with a note that happened to fall out of a crack between the stones of the Kosel directly into her hands. The note had been written by a woman who had a hearing-impaired young daughter. In the note, she asked Hashem to give her guidance and strength to deal with the girl's handicap.

My wife read the note to me. I asked her what "hearing impaired" meant; was it the same as being deaf? My wife said not quite; basically, hearing impaired meant half-deaf.

"Well then, what does she mean by 'give her guidance'?" I asked. "All she needs to do is to talk to her daughter in a louder-than-usual voice so she'll hear her."

"Her problem is not how the child will hear," my wife explained, "but what she should do about the fact that she has a daughter who doesn't hear well."

"What's the difference?" I asked.

"Maybe we should call them and invite them over for a visit?" my wife suggested.

"How would that help? I still say you should call her and tell her all she has to do is to shout a bit when she wants to say something to her daughter."

"No," my wife said firmly. "If she put the note in the wall, she must be having a hard time dealing with the situation, and we can help her."

Don't ask me how — my wife has her ways — but she succeeded in tracking down the woman from the note, and called her to invite her for lunch.

Of course, when my wife invited her, she had to come up with an explanation as to how she knew about the problem. She told the woman that a third-party had solicited her help, which is not altogether untrue. But to be honest, the only third-party involved was the Kosel itself, and I can guarantee you that not a single stone at the Kosel ever asked her to do anything. If it had, I would have been the first to know.

A young woman arrived accompanied by her five-year-old daughter, who was obviously the girl she had written about — she had big, bulky hearing-aids attached to each of her ears.

One of my daughters was also there at the time. Even though she's the mother of eight and has her own household to take care of, she comes over once a week to help my wife cook and serve a delicious lunch.

After everyone had finished eating, I told her that we had invited her over because we wanted to tell her a story — something that had happened to us personally.

The story is about one of my daughters, born forty years ago. Already during the first week, we noticed that something was wrong. When she was a few weeks old, we took her to the doctor. He examined her and told us our baby couldn't hear.

"You mean she's deaf?" I asked the doctor.

"Are you deaf?" my wife said to me. "That's exactly what the doctor said. She's deaf."

"No," I snapped, "all he said is that she can't hear!" I was pretty upset that my wife called me deaf and I wanted to give her a piece of my mind; but when I looked at her face I could see that she was not in a good mood, so I held my tongue.

We thanked the doctor and prepared to leave.

He looked at us strangely, and said, "I know this must be very upsetting for you. You're welcome to sit here awhile to recover from the shock."

"No thank you," I replied. "We'll recover at home. Now we're in a hurry to buy a blanket for the baby. Isn't it bad enough she's deaf; does she also have to be cold at night?"

The doctor asked me if I understood what it meant that my daughter was deaf.

"Of course I understand what it means," I replied. "It means she'll never hear a thing. But it's not the end of the world. With Hashem's help, she'll learn to deal with it."

We left his office, and started walking down the hallway that led to the entrance of the building. Half-way down, my wife asked me, "What do you do when a child is deaf?"

I told her I had no idea. This was the first time a child of mine had been born that way.

"Wait a minute," she said. "If she's deaf, how will she know what we're telling her?"

I told her that it was a good question and maybe we ought to go back and ask the doctor.

We went back to the doctor's office. He seemed a bit surprised to see us back so soon. When he heard our question, he looked flustered. "Listen," he said, "I understand your concern. But first you should go home and digest the news. Later I'll refer you to some top-notch professionals."

I told him that we had digested the bad news the moment he'd given it to us and besides, we weren't going home; hadn't I told him we were going to buy the baby a blanket? I suggested that maybe *he* had a hearing problem.

My wife told me not to be rude to the doctor, but I told her that I just wanted a simple answer to an even simpler question.

Realizing that it would be wise to answer my question if he planned on getting any more work done that day, the doctor told us that since our daughter couldn't hear we would have to communicate with her through sign language. It was also possible to teach her to read lips.

I asked if she needed eardrops or anything like that. "Nothing," he said. "I'll set up an appointment for you with a doctor who'll explain everything you need to know."

We bought a blanket and returned home.

When we told our oldest child (we had only four, then) that the baby was deaf, he asked, "Does that mean that when she's sleeping I don't have to worry about being quiet and I can make as much noise as I want?"

We managed to outsmart our daughter's deafness, and she blossomed beautifully. Instead of talking to her, we would show her an object and make up hand signals for it. She ended up receiving more attention than any other child in the family, or any other child in Meah Shearim, for that matter.

She was such a bright and pretty child. My wife dressed her beautifully, and she received admiring looks from all the neighbors whenever she went out. We were so proud of her.

When she was about three years old, we registered her for kindergarten. One day, a short while after that, when my wife was shopping in Geulah, a saleswoman asked my daughter where she was going for kindergarten. My daughter signaled with her hands that she was deaf.

"Is she going to a special school for deaf children?" the saleswoman asked my wife.

"Why would I send her to a special school?" my wife responded. "She's going to Morah Fruma (the kindergarten teacher in the regular school)."

"You mean Fruma agreed to accept her?" the saleswoman wondered. "Maybe she doesn't know that your daughter is deaf?"

My wife realized that the saleswoman couldn't possibly be from Meah Shearim because everyone knew that Morah Fruma knew everything that happened in the neighborhood. If our daughter had been missing a toenail on her pinky toe, Fruma would have known about it.

Besides, there was no such thing as Fruma not accepting a child into her kindergarten. So what if a child was deaf, or blind or whatever? Hers was a Meah Shearim kindergarten, wasn't it?

When our daughter completed kindergarten, she attended the local Bais Yaakov, where she was a regular student, even one of the best in her class. She would bring home lots of friends, and let me tell you, they were as loud as she was quiet.

She was such a pleasant little girl that she made friends with everybody. I do remember one time, though, that the teacher told my wife that there was one girl in the class who was very sad because my daughter didn't want to be her friend. The teacher asked the child what made her say so and the little girl replied that my daughter never listened to her. The teacher explained that although my daughter couldn't hear, that didn't mean she wasn't listening.

My daughter grew up, graduated high school and reached marriageable age. I called a *shadchan* and asked, "Tell me, maybe you have a *bachur* for my daughter?"

"What are you looking for?" he asked. "Tall or short; someone who wants to stay in learning or a working boy?"

"Listen," I said, "you know my daughter is wonderful girl. But let's face it, she's deaf. So, it doesn't really matter to me what the boy looks like or whether he's a *talmid chacham*. I just want a good boy for my daughter, someone who's willing to marry a deaf girl."

The *shadchan* told me that he liked the fact that I didn't think I was who-knows-what and that I wasn't being picky. I told him that actually I did think I was who-knows-what but that I was just being realistic.

It wasn't long before he suggested a *shidduch* with a good boy, who sat and learned. His family didn't have such a good name and normally we wouldn't have considered him for one of our daughters. Don't get me wrong, he was a nice boy with good *middos*, and I liked him the moment I met him. But my daughter had an excellent name as a pretty, sociable, talented girl, and some of our neighbors felt that we could have done better. But what did I care what people thought?

They had a beautiful wedding. Some people said they saw me cry a few tears at the *chuppah*. It's possible. I have a real soft spot in my heart for this quiet daughter of mine. You know what they say, still waters enter everywhere, or something like that.

During the *Sheva Berachos*, various *rabbanim* gave speeches in praise of the *chasan* and *kallah*. They all mentioned me and my wife, as well, and spoke about how we had raised our daughter like any other normal child. They went on and on about how proud we'd always been of her and how we didn't let her handicap keep her from being like everyone else.

On the fourth day of *Sheva Berachos*, after our *rav* gave his speech, again heaping praises on me and my wife, a few of the guests called out that I should stand up and say a few words. As you know, I don't usually talk a lot. I mean, I do, but not in public. But this was too much.

I stood up and said, "You're praising me for raising as a normal child the smartest, easiest, prettiest and best daughter one could wish for. I don't understand, do you think that I would be ashamed of her? Well, let me tell you: I wish that all of you here would have such a special daughter! Who cares that she's deaf?"

I saw that everyone was crying so I decided that I better stop talking before the happy event would turn into a sad one. After that, no one heaped praises on us anymore, as if we were something special. Instead, they spoke about how special the *kallah* was.

After the week of *Sheva Berachos*, the young couple began building their family. It wasn't long before they were blessed with one child after another, all of them healthy and with perfect hearing.

When their first child was born, I told my son-in-law jokingly, "Look what a good thing: he hears *and* he's from a good family!" I could tell that he didn't take my good-natured comment that well; I think he was a little hurt. Right then I decided I wouldn't repeat it when future children were born. I almost always kept my word.

After I finished my story, I saw that the woman was crying. I concluded by saying, "You shouldn't spend all your time worrying about your daughter's small problem, be happy that she's healthy and has eyes and a face and hands and feet, and even ears that you can put hearing devices into."

She seemed very happy as she rose and thanked us for inviting her. She thanked me for the story and my wife and daughter for the delicious meal. She complimented us on the fact that we had such devoted daughters who gave us so much *nachas* and came to help us.

We walked to the door and just as she was about to leave, she turned around suddenly and said, "Maybe you can arrange for me to meet your daughter... the one who's deaf? I'd like to see her with my own eyes."

"Of course," my wife said. "Why did I invite you on Tuesday, the day Yochi comes over? Please meet Yochi, who helped me cook and serve everything. She's our daughter, forty years old and the mother of eight beautiful children. She's the deaf daughter you wanted to meet."

That is my story, Rabbi Walder, and you should tell it to anyone who has a handicapped child.

My wife says to tell you and your readers that slowly but surely you'll get to know our entire family — but there's plenty of time for that.

# A Fish Story

I work for a taxi company in Bnei Brak and have been driving my cab for over twenty-five years.

Any taxi driver can tell you enough stories to fill an encyclopedia. Some of them are true, and some just might be true if you stretch your imagination a little.

Well, fishermen have their fish stories, but I bet you never heard a fish story from a taxi driver before. What I'm about to tell is one hundred percent true, and you can check it out. It happened at the end of the month of Elul.

I'm told to pick up a local fare; someone wants to go to Tel HaShomer Hospital. I go to the address, and I see a woman standing there with a bucket. No mop, just a bucket.

She opens the taxi door and starts to put the bucket on the front seat.

Now, I've had a lot of different people in my taxi, and they've loaded, or tried to load, all sorts of weird objects into my cab. So I've learned to be pretty tolerant over the years, and I really have no objection to buckets *per se*. But I draw the line at buckets filled almost to the brim with water.

"Hey, hey," I say to the lady. "What do you think you're doing? With all due respect, I can't take a bucket full of water in my cab. Why don't you put it in empty, and fill it when you get where you're going?"

What does she say to me? "But mister, there's a fish in this bucket."

This is getting weird.

"Ma'am," I say, "in this cab, I take only dead fish and live people. No live fish in buckets are going anywhere with me."

"Oh, please," she says. "Do it as a special favor. It's a big mitzvah."

I want to know *exactly* what mitzvah I'm performing by schlepping a fish in a bucket in my cab, and she says, "My father is very sick. He's in a hospice next to Tel HaShomer, and he could pass away at any moment. So I thought, 'What can I possibly do for him before he dies…'"

"So you're bringing him a fish? That's a *wonderful* idea! I'm sure he'll enjoy it to no end."

"This is no time for sarcasm," she says reproachfully. "My father can't eat the fish; he's been on a feeding tube for a year already."

"So what's it for, then? A pet?"

"Of course not," she says. "It's for *kapparos*. I started to tell you that I wanted to do something for him. I decided that the only thing I can give him now is a *kapparah* before he leaves this world."

I stop laughing at her, and start thinking how I might be able to arrange this. "All right," I say. "Put it on the floor here next to me. I'll clean up the water later."

She puts down the bucket and gets in. I start the meter. I've wasted ten minutes already. The dispatcher's voice comes over the speaker; he wants to know where I am now. "I'm just leaving for Tel HaShomer," I say. He grumbles something about how it's taking me awfully long and asks me to let him know as soon as I'm free.

After driving for about ten minutes, I hear the woman say, "*Oy vey!*"

"What's wrong?" I ask her.

"I don't know if the fish is male or female!"

"What does it matter?"

"For *kapparos* you need a male fish for a man, and a female for a woman. My father's a man (I'm so glad she told me that, or I wouldn't have known), so I have to bring him a male fish."

"So what are you going to do?"

"I'll just have to call the fish store and ask them if they sold me a male fish or a female."

"Okay, so call."

"Have you got a cell phone?" she asks.

I should have seen that coming. Every taxi driver just *loves* passengers who want to make just one little call on their personal cell phone. I can't explain it; it's just a warm, tender feeling that develops over the years.

"Okay, what's the number?" I ask through clenched teeth.

"Call information; then you'll know," she says serenely.

Just one little call? I see that this business is really going to run up my phone bill.

I find out the number of Mottel's Fish Market and make the call. I have the speaker on, so the lady can hear both sides of the conversation.

"Hi," I say. "Um, there's a lady here who bought a fish from you about half an hour ago."

"Mister, there were about twenty-five ladies buying fish here about half an hour ago."

"It's me, the one with the bucket!" she yells from the back-seat. "Do you remember me?"

Does he remember? How could he forget?

"So what's the problem, ma'am?"

"Did you sell me a male fish, or a female?"

I hear a guffaw over the line. "Did you hear that, Shimon? The lady with the bucket wants to know if her fish is male or female." Now I hear about five people laughing in the background.

"Lady, we're not zoologists. We just sell fish; we don't check if they're male or female, unless someone asks us to."

"So what do we do now, feller?" I ask quietly.

He tells me how to check if the fish is male or female.

I get out of the car, take the bucket, put it on the hood, and start the investigation. Just then, Maurice, another driver from the company, comes along. "Is everything okay?" he asks, slowing down to a halt.

Feeling sort of embarrassed, I say, "Yeah, everything's fine; I'm just checking if this fish is male or female."

Maurice gives me a funny look. He starts moving, then stops again and says, "Are you *sure* everything's all right?"

I don't need this. I'm annoyed enough already. "Don't worry about me," I tell him. "Just give me a break this time and let me do what I have to do here."

Maurice gives me another questioning look, but then continues driving, leaving me alone to try and grab the slippery fish in the bucket.

And then I remember that you're not supposed to touch raw fish with your bare hands, because it might be contaminated with deadly germs. So I put the bucket back into the cab and start driving.

"So what is it, male or female?" the lady wants to know.

I explain that I wasn't able to find that out yet. "Let me

get to a place where they have plastic bags," I say, "so I'll have something to protect my hands."

"But didn't you touch the fish already?"

"Ma'am," I say, barely hanging on to my patience. "Allow me to check the fish under sanitary conditions."

I hear my own voice, but I can hardly believe my ears. A taxi driver for twenty-five years, and I'm talking about sanitary conditions. I can't believe that I got mixed up in such a bizarre situation.

I stop at a vegetable store. Again, I take out the bucket and put it on the hood. I take some plastic bags from the vegetable stand, and cover my hands with them.

The greengrocer comes running out of the store. "What do you think you're doing?" he yells. "Those bags are for my customers!"

"There's a woman here who's taking a fish to her father," I explain, summoning up all my dignity, "and I have to check if it's male or female."

"What is this, mister, some kind of joke?"

"Come and see for yourself."

Before I know it, I've got an audience of two greengrocers and half a dozen customers. I get hold of the fish and start pressing on it like the fish fellow told me to. As far as I'm concerned, I've had my *kapparah* already. My cell phone rings. It's the dispatcher. "What's the story with you?" he demands. "I've been calling you on the radio, why aren't you answering?"

"I'm outside the cab at the moment," I say. "I've got this fish here, and I have to check if it's male or female."

"Oh, so you're pulling my leg now, are you? All right, Yitz. Run along and play nicely. Just wait; you'll see how soon I send you to pick up another fare. I'm reporting you for disciplinary action."

For some reason, he took my answer as a joke, and what's more, he took it personally. If there are Ten Commandments for taxi drivers, the first commandment is "Thou shalt not make fun at the dispatcher's expense."

Meanwhile, I'm surrounded by admiring onlookers who seem to think I just landed from Mars.

Then a woman comes out of the vegetable store and saves the day. "Let me have a look," she says. "I'll tell you what it is in a jiffy." She takes hold of the fish and announces, "It's a female."

That's great. That's just great.

"What now?" I ask my passenger.

"We go back to Bnei Brak, and I buy another fish," she says.

Silently, I get behind the wheel and drive back to Bnei Brak. On the way, I try to contact the office over the radio. No answer. Total silence. I know what that means, but I don't say anything to the lady. What good would it do?

We go into the fish store, and they dump the fish back into the tank. I warn the guy behind the counter that this time, we want a real he-man fish. He drops a big, muscular-looking specimen into the bucket, and we go back to the taxi. I put the bucket up front, and off we go to the hospice.

All the way there, she keeps telling me over and over how grateful she is and what a big mitzvah I'm doing. I don't answer her; I just hope I won't have to pay too high a price for the mitzvah. I remember reading that if you're on your way to do a mitzvah, you won't come to harm, and that's what I'm counting on now.

By the time I park the cab in front of the hospice, I feel personally involved in this business with the fish, and I say to the lady, "I'll carry the bucket; it's pretty heavy." She doesn't ar-gue with me, and we go up to the entrance. There, wouldn't you know, we come up against a burly Russian security guard.

"What's that you carry there?" he asks.

"Nothing," I say. "Just a fish." He looks at me as if I was an alien. I don't mind, I'm used to it by now.

"A wash pail with fish you wish to bring into hospice?" he asks.

"That's right, sir. This lady is bringing this fish to her fa-ther."

He looks at us sternly. "No fishes for fathers. Against rules of hospice."

I start arguing with him. I wasn't born yesterday, and I find it hard to believe the hospice has a rule on its books against bringing fish in buckets into the facility.

"I'll go to the head nurse," the lady suggests, "and ask her to give me permission to bring it in."

She goes inside, and I'm left at the doorstep like a fool, holding a bucket with a fish that keeps looking up and laugh-ing at me. I wait for five minutes, ten minutes. Every few sec-onds I make eye contact with the security guard, whose look seems to say, "Head nurse not give permission. Go home with fish," or something like that.

It's been twenty minutes already. I've already wasted two hours on this ridiculous business, and there's still no end in sight.

Half an hour. I guess that lady's never coming out of there.

I glance around, all jittery, and what do I see? There's a goldfish pond, just a few yards away.

I look at my watch again, and I peer through the glass doors. She still isn't coming. I've had all I can take. I take the bucket over to the fishpond and dump the fish with a nice big splash. That feels better.

Then the Russian guard is screaming, "You are crazy man, throw big fish into goldfish pond?! Might be sick fish! Might eat up little fish!"

And the next thing you know, he's got his shoes and socks off, and he's in the pool barking into his walkie-talkie. Another guard comes running out of the hospice, pulls off his shoes, and jumps in, too. They're both in there trying to catch the he-man fish.

I guess it's pretty funny, but I'm in no mood for laughter. I sit there at the edge of the pool with the empty bucket, waiting for them to catch the fish.

Finally they catch it and throw it back into the bucket, and just then the lady comes running out, half crying, "They won't give me permission to bring in the fish. I'm so sorry I kept you waiting all this time; my father's about to die and I was saying *Viduy* and *Shema Yisrael* with him."

I thrust the bucket into her hands and whisper, "Quick, go and do *kapparos* on your father. Don't look back. I'll stop them from coming after you."

The security guards are looking for their socks. She gets the picture and dashes through the sliding doors before they can stop her. Barefoot, they start chasing her, but I jump in front of the entrance and block it with all my might.

What can I say? These Russians are tough; they start hitting me to make me let go. I don't hit back — not that I don't know how to fight, but I don't want to let go of those doorposts for a second. I'm not planning on letting them get past me, so I just let them hit me.

They call the police, and in a couple of minutes, two cops arrive and tell me to get out of the way. When I tell them that I'm not going to budge from that spot, each one grabs one of my wrists and they physically lift me up and fling me to the ground (interesting that the Russians hadn't thought of doing that). They all run inside, and I quickly jump up and start running after them, yelling, "Leave her alone, she just wants to do *kapparos*!"

It's a crazy scene in a hospice full of dying people. Five guys running down the hall and yelling — two barefoot security guards, two cops, and a taxi driver, trying to stop all four of them. They open door after door on the first floor, but don't find the woman.

Then they go up to the second floor and begin checking all the rooms. When they open the fourth door, something makes them stop in their tracks.

There's the lady with the bucket raised in her hands, standing over a frail, motionless old man in bed, crying bitterly and swinging the bucket around in circles, saying "*Zeh kaparascha, zeh chalifascha...*"

Luckily for her, I've managed to delay them until the last moment. She's just finishing the third round. She puts the bucket down on the floor, bends over the old man, strokes his cheek and says, "*Tatty, Tatty...*now you're cleansed completely. I did *kapparos* for you. You can die without suffering now."

The old man doesn't answer, but we all see two big tears squeeze out of his eyes and roll down the side of his cheeks.

I also feel a little wet around the eyes. It must be water that splashed on me from the goldfish pond. But I see that the two policemen are also crying. The Russians aren't crying, but they look pretty stunned.

The old man starts breathing heavily. A nurse comes in just at that moment and asks us to clear the way. She looks at the monitors and says to the lady, "These are his last moments. Is there something you want to say to him?"

"I want ten men here to say *Shema Yisrael* with him," says the lady.

There are five of us already. We run out to the corridor and collect five more. The ten of us, eight of whom are Jews for sure, find something to put on our heads, and the lady says to us, "Repeat after me: *Shema Yisrael*..." We say all the prayers she tells us to say, and right after that, the old man takes his last breath. The nurse checks his pulse. She pulls the sheet over his head and turns to the woman. "I'm sorry," she says, "he's gone."

We all file out of the room. As we're walking out, one of the cops pats me on the shoulder and says, "Are you okay, feller? You aren't injured are you?"

"It's all right, brother," I tell him. "You did what you thought was right," and we give each other a little hug.

The security guards clap me on the shoulder, too. I go over and ask the lady if there's anything I can do to help. She asks me to call her husband and tell him to come. I make the call, and they decide that she'll stay there while he makes the funeral arrangements.

I ask her if I can leave now. She says thank you, thank you and that I have a big mitzvah to my credit because her father had been a *tzaddik*, and now he's left this world happy and pure — and with a *kapparah*, thanks to me. She starts crying again, and I'm feeling pretty choked up myself.

She asks how much she owes me, and I refuse to take a penny from her. For some reason I've been chosen to take part in this whole strange business and I feel like it was all meant to be.

I start walking away, and suddenly I hear her calling after me, "Driver, driver!"

I turn around, and she's standing there with the bucket in her hand.

"Take the fish," she says. "You should eat it at the meal before the Yom Kippur fast."

I tell her that I'm afraid to take it. I just can't, I feel like I have a personal bond with that fish; how can I eat it? So she says, "Give it to a needy family, then."

I take the bucket and leave the hospice. I'm tempted to just throw the fish away somewhere, but I don't have the nerve to do it. I feel like there is something holy about that fish.

I'm just pulling out of the hospital grounds when a Chassid flags me down. "Can you take me to Bnei Brak?"

I nod. He opens the door to get into the front seat, and then sees the bucket with the fish in it.

"Sit in the backseat," I tell him.

I could see his enthusiasm is dampened. The look on his face tells me that he's reconsidering whether he wants to ride with me. But I guess he doesn't want to offend me, and he gets into the backseat.

"I guess you're wondering about this fish here," I say. "This is a story you've got to hear."

I start telling him the whole story, and in the meantime we reach his destination in Bnei Brak, and I'm still talking and talking. The Chassid is all ears.

"I want you to wait for me here," he says, all excited. "No, on second thought, I want you to come in with me and tell this story to my Rebbe."

Next thing I know, I'm in the house of a very famous Chassidic Rebbe.

There are a lot of people in the waiting room, but my Chassid takes the *gabbai* aside and starts whispering something into his ear. The *gabbai* keeps looking at me while the

Chassid is talking. He then comes up to me says, "Go right in, both of you."

I go inside with the Chassid. The Rebbe is sitting there. I can see right away he's a very holy man. The Chassid says a few words to him in Yiddish, and then asks me to tell the story over in Hebrew.

I don't want to take up too much of his time, so I tell him the main points of the story, with a few highlights, including the delays on the way. The Rebbe listens closely, and at some points he smiles. He even laughs at one point. But when I get to the end, where the lady is doing the *kapparos*, he suddenly starts to cry.

He's literally sobbing. His whole body is shaking, tears are streaming from his eyes. The Rebbe tries to compose himself, but then he starts crying again.

Finally he says to me, in broken Hebrew, in between sobs, "I am in very stormy spirits lately because of the state this generation is in; I hardly ever have time to receive people, I'm so fearful of the approaching days of judgment. And now you come to me with this story, and it gives me great encouragement. I see how, after all the difficulties and obstacles, an elderly Jew merited his *kapparah* moments before his death, so why should we be without hope? I have a request to make of you: Allow me to eat this fish at the *seudah mafsekes*; it will elevate the soul of that elderly man and serve to bring pardon and atonement to this entire generation. In the merit of your gift, I will pray for your success."

Well I'm glad to leave the fish there; I feel like a burden has been lifted from me.

I drive to the taxi stand, and on the way, I hear the loudspeakers already announcing the old man's funeral. At the taxi stand, I tell the dispatcher and all the drivers what happened. They all get a little damp around the eyes and agree to put something on their heads to say some *Tehillim* with me in memory of the deceased. A few even want to take part in the funeral.

All this happened just a few days ago, and I decided I ought to publicize this story. I guess you're the right man for that job.

I hope the Jewish People will merit *selichah* and *kapparah*, and may this be a good year for all of *Am Yisrael*.

# Glossary

The following glossary provides a partial explanation of some of the Hebrew, Yiddish (Y.), and Aramaic (A.) words and phrases used in this book. The spellings and explanations reflect the way the specific word is used herein. Often, there are alternate spellings and meanings for the words.

**ALIYAH:** lit., "ascent"; immigration to Israel.

**AM YISRAEL:** the Nation of Israel.

**BA'AL TESHUVAH:** a formerly non-observant Jew who has returned to Jewish tradition and practice.

**BACHUR:** a young man; a yeshivah student.

**BARUCH HASHEM:** "Thank God!"

**BEDEKEN:** (Y.) lit., "veiling"; at the beginning of the wedding ceremony, a groom covers his bride with her veil.

**BEIN HAZMANIM:** the "vacation" days between one yeshivah semester and another.

**BEIS DIN:** a rabbinical court of law.

**BEIS MIDRASH:** the study hall of a yeshivah.

**BERACHAH:** blessing.

**CHAREIDI:** an ultra-Orthodox Jew.

**CHASAN:** a bridegroom.

**CHAVRUSA:** (A.) a Torah study partner.

**CHAZAL:** an acronym for "our Sages, of blessed memory."

**CHAZZAN:** cantor.

**CHESED:** acts of kindness.

**CHEVREMAN:** (Y.) an easygoing person; "one of the guys."

**CHIZUK:** strengthening and encouragement.

**CHUPPAH:** a wedding canopy; a wedding.

**DAVEN:** (Y.) pray.

**EISHES CHAYIL:** "a woman of valor," from *Mishlei* 31:10–31.

**GABBAI:** a synagogue officer.

**GADOL:** lit., "great"; a Torah authority.

**GEDOLEI HADOR:** leading Torah authorities of the generation.

**GET:** a Jewish bill of divorce.

**HAKADOSH BARUCH HU:** the Holy One, Blessed be He.

**HASHEM:** God.

**HASHGACHAH PRATIS:** Divine Providence.

**HAVDALAH:** the blessing recited at the conclusion of Shabbos and Festivals, separating the holy day from the other days of the week.

**KADDISH:** a prayer sanctifying God's Name; the mourner's prayer.

**KALLAH:** a bride.

**KAPPARAH:** atonement.

**KAPPAROS:** the custom of waiving fish/chicken/money three times over one's head to achieve an atonement prior to Yom Kippur.

**KAVANAH:** intention; concentration.

**KEHILLAH:** a community.

**KEVER:** a grave.

**KEVOD SHAMAYIM:** the honor of Heaven.

**KO'ACH:** power; strength.

**KOLLEL:** a center for advanced Torah study for adult students, mostly married men.

**L'CHAIM:** lit., "to life!"; a toast.

**MAARIV:** the evening prayer service.

**MECHILAH:** forgiveness.

**MECHITZAH:** a divider.

**MESADER KIDDUSHIN:** the one who conducts the Jewish wedding ceremony.

**MIDDOS:** [good] character traits.

# Glossary

**MIKVEH:** an immersion pool for ritual purification.

**MINCHAH:** the afternoon prayer service.

**MOTZA'EI SHABBOS:** Saturday night, after Shabbos ends.

**NACHAS:** pride; pleasure.

**NEBACH:** (Y.) a person to be pitied.

**RABBANIM:** rabbis.

**SEFER TEHILLIM:** the Book of Psalms.

**SELICHAH:** pardon.

**SEUDAH MAFSEKES:** the meal preceding a fast.

**SEUDAS HODA'AH:** a festive meal of thanksgiving that one makes after surviving a life-threatening illness/accident/calamity.

**SHACHARIS:** the morning prayer service.

**SHADCHAN:** a matchmaker.

**SHEMA YISRAEL:** "Hear O Israel..." (*Devarim* 6:5), the opening words of the fundamental Jewish prayer which proclaims the Unity of God.

**SHEVA BERACHOS:** the seven blessings recited at a wedding; any of the festive meals held in honor of the bride and groom during the week following the wedding, at which the seven blessings are recited.

**SHIDDUCH(IM):** marital match(es).

**SHIVAH:** the seven-day period of mourning.

**SIMCHAH:** joy; a joyous occasion.

**TALMID CHACHAM:** a Torah scholar.

**TEFILLIN:** phylacteries.

**TEHILLIM:** the Book of Psalms.

**TENAYIM:** lit., "stipulations"; the written agreement made when a couple becomes engaged.

**TESHUVAH:** repentance.

**TZADDIK:** a pious, righteous man.

**TZADEIKES:** (Y.) a pious, righteous woman.

**VIDUY:** the confessional prayer.

**VORT:** (Y.) lit., "a word"; a short Torah discourse; celebration of a couple's engagement.

**YAHRTZEIT:** (Y.) the anniversary of a death.

**YARMULKE:** (Y.) a skullcap.

**YEKKE:** a Jew of Germanic descent.

**YESHIVAH BACHUR(IM):** yeshivah student(s).

**YESHIVAH GEDOLAH:** a Torah academy for teenage boys.

**YESHIVAH KETANAH:** a Torah academy for post-high-school-age boys.

**YID:** (Y.) Jew.

**ZIVUG:** predestined marriage partner.